A RETREAT FOR LAY PEOPLE

A Retreat For Lay People

Spiritual Guidance for Christian Living

RONALD KNOX

IGNATIUS PRESS SAN FRANCISCO

Nihil obstat: Hubertus Richards, S.T.L., L.S.S., *Censor Deputatus*
Imprimatur: E. Morrogh Bernard, *Vic. Gen.*
Westmonasterii, die 4A Decembris, 1954

Cover design by Riz Boncan Marsella

Published in 2011 by Ignatius Press, San Francisco

ISBN 978-1-58617-592-4
Library of Congress Control Number 2010937200
Printed in the United States of America ♾

TO MAGDALEN ELDON

CONTENTS

PREFACE

There are, I suppose, two ways of conducting a retreat, I mean, of preparing those meditations which are the bones of a retreat. One is to take a single idea which will run like a thread through all the meditations and bind them together, make them into a coherent whole. The other is to seize upon an idea here, an idea there, as they occur to you in the intervals of prayer or in the course of reading, work it out there and then, and lay it by for future use. This means that you have a stockpot of meditations from which you can select the items which seem most appropriate to the occasion; but the framework of your retreat will be of the flimsiest.

"The Retreat for Priests", which I published eight years ago, was of the former kind—was, as you may say, a strategic retreat. It followed the course of Old Testament history, finding types everywhere to illustrate, and in some sort of order, the familiar themes of Christian piety. The present volume makes no such claim to organic unity. I have simply put together certain samples of the meditations I have been giving, these fifteen years back; they are not of a pattern. But I doubt whether there is any need to apologize for this cavalier procedure. When you are in retreat, it is always difficult to find *the* book you want; there is a daintiness in your spiritual tastes which calls for the meal à la carte, rather than the table d'hôte. All the better, then, if you light on a work which leaves you free to pick and choose, instead of following the whim of your author. There is room for books which offer a varied menu to the retreatant.

Some of these meditations were designed partly, though not exclusively, for school-boy audiences, and are simpler than the rest. Some were written during the war years, when the repercussion of public events was felt more deeply than it is at present. In any case, they represent a series of moods, not a single, fixed mood, on the part of the author; and this allows him to hope that one here, one there will chime in with the mood of the reader.

At the same time, they have not been thrown together at haphazard; they are so arranged as to fit in, more or less, with the traditional lines laid down in the *Spiritual Exercises*. They fall into three groups of eight; of these, the first represents the "foundations"; the second is based on the life and death of our Blessed Lord; the third envisages practical, day-to-day needs. Between the first group and the second, and again between the second group and the third, I have thrown out suggestions which might be useful to those who are following the devotion of the Holy Hour.

To those who have asked, at Grayshott and elsewhere, whether I meant to publish "my retreat", I have fulfilled a promise.

MELLS, Feast of Saint Ignatius, 1954

I

DISCOURAGEMENT IN RETREAT

The Gospels tell us curiously little about the machinery of our Lord's life on earth—I mean, about the houses he actually lived in, the rooms he actually took his meals in, when he was not taking his meals or passing the night on the open mountainside. Again and again we are told that he was "in the house"—what house? His own, or somebody else's? And if so, whose? True, at the beginning of Saint John, two disciples want to go and see where he dwells; he invites them there, and they spend all the day with him, but never a word about this dwelling-place of his; Saint John doesn't tell us what it was like when they got there. Once, and once only, we are let into the secret of our Lord's arrangements, and the description we are given makes them more mysterious than ever. It is on the eve of his Passion: "He sent two of his disciples [we are told] on an errand: Go into the city, and there a man will meet you, carrying a jar of water; you are to follow him, and say to the owner of the house into which he enters, The Master says, Where is my room, in which I am to eat the paschal meal with my disciples? And he will show you a large upper room, furnished and prepared; it is there that you are to make ready for us." Some forty days later, after the Ascension, we are told that the disciples "went up into the upper room, where they dwelt", all eleven of them; "all these, with one mind, gave themselves up to prayer, together with Mary the mother of Jesus, and the rest of the women, and his brethren". It is natural, I think, to suppose that the same upper room is meant—the whole upper floor of some fairly large house, which our Lord's followers used as their place of assembly, and probably as their living quarters, whenever they found themselves in Jerusalem between the Last Supper and the Day of Pentecost.

If so, what memories it must have had for them! A haunted room, that had witnessed so much of a brief but poignant history! You may call it, if you will, a drama in five acts. The first act was the Last Supper itself. There, on that table, they had rested the plate of bread, the cup of wine, over which the words of mystery had been uttered. Through that door, pursued by questioning glances, the traitor had slunk out into the night. Those walls still echoed with the accents of the remembered voice: "After a little while, you will see me no longer, and again after a little while you will have sight of me, because I am going back to the Father." Memories of foreboding and bewilderment, of dark suspicions, and of high resolve.

Of the second act, the Gospels tell us nothing; the omission is not difficult to account for. But I suppose the disciples, when they fled from Gethsemani, will have found their way, little hunted parties of them, back to the Cenacle. Where else should they go, in Jerusalem? Whom should they trust, now that one of their own number had turned renegade? In little groups, avoiding one another's eyes, they crept back to their old rendezvous—the men who had boasted, a few hours back, that they were ready to die with their Master. Only one is missing; what has become of Simon Peter? Was he, after all, as good as his word? And then the door opens once again, and the tale of their defection is complete; Simon Peter has come in, his face furrowed with tears—memories of shame and of defeat, of a time when all was lost, and their honour was lost too.

Easter morning had come and gone, but the same imaginary fears persisted. They are still behind locked doors at the opening of the third act, on the Sunday evening. But their fears are mingled with a strange excitement; the body of their Master no longer rests in its grave, and stories are being told of lonely encounters with him, in the pale light of dawn, the fading light of dusk; are they, after all, to see him again? If so, it will not be here; his own message is clear about that: "He is going on before you into *Galilee*, where you shall have sight of him." Not here, in the theatre of their defeat, among the memories of their shame, but on the hill-slopes of Galilee, restored to the innocence of their first conversion, they will be able to meet him and look him in the face. All at once, they are conscious of a newcomer in their midst, one for whom locked gates without, locked doors within, are no barrier—it must be a spirit! But no, it is their Master himself; there are scars on hands and feet; in matter-of-fact tones, he asks them if they have any food handy; he eats and drinks before them. Memories of excitement and alarm, of relief and sudden rejoicing.

And now we have reached the fourth act of the drama, the last before that final dénouement of Pentecost. They have come back from the hill-brow of the Ascension; their eyes ache with looking towards their God, as he was taken up out of their sight, and the relentless heavens closed behind him. "Coming in, they went up into the upper room where they dwelt, Peter and John, James and Andrew, Philip and Thomas, Bartholomew and Matthew, James the son of Alphaeus and Simon the Zealot, and Judas the brother of James"—the familiar company; can you not detect a slight weariness in Saint Luke's manner as he calls the roll we all know by heart? They came back to their familiar surroundings and take up again the burden of day-to-day living. There are routine tasks to be got through; a vacancy in the number of the twelve demands the appointment of a successor to Judas Iscariot. When that is done, they give themselves up to prayer; how dull, how flat prayer itself seems now, when they have no longer at their side the Master who prayed *with* them, have not yet received into their hearts the Spirit who will pray *in* them! It is no longer a living inspiration, but a thankless exercise. "Our Father, who art in heaven"—but heaven is not content with that; it has claimed the sacred humanity as well. "Thy kingdom come"—but what signs are there that it is coming? Heaven has opened and shut again, and the miserable life of mankind goes on. "Give us this day our daily bread"—but who, now, is to break for them that supersubstantial bread for which their appetite has been quickened? "And forgive us our trespasses"—but where is the gracious voice that once assured them of forgiveness? How empty, how desolate the world feels when we have been robbed, by death or by separation, of somebody with whom we were accustomed to share, and to enjoy it! How every memory of the past turns to a regret, because that chapter is closed! And to the disciples, I imagine, that prayer in the Cenacle must have felt lifeless and insipid, all the more because the Cenacle was a haunted room for them, impregnated with the vivid history of their immediate past.

"Together with Mary"—ah, that is what we were waiting for! Something still made the Cenacle a home for those dispirited hearts; so much heaven had taken away from them, but it had left them a hostage, a keepsake, in place of their Master; part (you might almost say) of himself. She, more than any of the others, was bereaved; her memories went back further, much further, than theirs. Had she not borne him in her womb, nursed him in her arms, fondled him on her knee; had she not ministered to the needs of the Almighty, watched wonder dawn in the eyes of the Omniscient? Those others had followed him; she had lived for him. To them, the walls of the Cenacle were haunted by regrets; for her, there was no sight on earth which did not remind her of her loss; these thirty years, she had hung on his lips, seen with his eyes. Yet in her face there is no shadow of dejection; the angels who announced her Son's departure from this earth could win from her no other echo than the angel who announced his coming to it: "Behold the handmaid of the Lord; let it be unto me according to thy word."

Those nine days between Ascension Day and Pentecost, the first of all the novenas—shall we go back to them sometimes, to find consolation about our own difficulties in prayer? I doubt if there is anything which puts us back so much—I am speaking of ordinary Christians—about the practice of religion, as the sense of staleness. And this comes from a defect in ourselves, which is a natural defect. The human animal is so built, that the more poignant emotions do not last; as time goes on, their edge is blunted by mere familiarity. Go and settle down in some part of the country which has always appealed to you as having a special atmosphere of mystery or of romance, and before you have lived there six months it is mysterious, it is romantic, no longer. Hear some melody that enchants you with its novelty, and by the time it is on all the gramophones you will be stopping your ears against the sound of it. Even the experience of a great love disappoints us; it has its law of diminishing returns, and no marriage can be a perpetual honeymoon. We recognize that law, but for some reason we do not expect it to apply in the matter of our emotional response to religion. We converts especially, in the first years of our conversion, cannot bring ourselves to believe that this inheritance into which we have come, with its splendid liturgy, its delicately balanced theological system, its tender refinements of devotion, will ever become staled for us by use. But the years go on and take their unconscious toll of us; we are men, and seven times pass over us; we look back, in some moment of reflexion, and discover that all is not with us as yesterday and the day before.

And I think it is useful to remember all that in time of retreat, perhaps especially when we are standing on the threshold of a retreat. We experience at such times, many of us, a curious kind of depression. Well, I suppose a retreat is meant to be depressing; it's going into a tunnel and hoping to see light at the other end; but we get, I think, the wrong kind of depression about it, if we are not careful. It is not the sins we are to repent of, it is not the bad habits we are to conquer, that stand out in our minds. Rather, it is a sense of overall staleness, of the kind I have been describing. You were vaguely conscious of it before, but you thought it would be all right when you went into retreat; alone with yourself you would recover, easily enough, the vivid sense of God's presence; prayer would come easy to you. And instead of that, going into retreat only makes you more conscious than ever that the thought of God is distant, that prayer is a laborious exercise—just so, a man who has had a dull toothache all day will promise himself relief when he goes to bed, only to find the ache more insistent now that he has nothing else to think about, now that he is alone with it. Think of some retreat you have attended. You'd taken some book out of the library, carefully chosen for the occasion, by some author whose spirit you found attractive; and now, suddenly, it had lost its charm for you. The exercises of the retreat—the Stations of the Cross, for example—got on your nerves; they seemed rhetorical and overstrained. The public meditations didn't hit off your mood; they may have been all very well for some people, you felt, but they hadn't gotten your wave-length; they were just words to you. And as the days of the retreat began to slip away, you felt thoroughly miserable; this great opportunity of grace offered you, and you could make nothing of it; you could only sit there moping and criticizing. Just when you would have liked to be at your best, you found yourself in low gear. Probably, as I have been saying, that is what happened to the holy apostles during those vital days of their ordination retreat in the Cenacle. They weren't at their best; how could they be at their best, left alone in a Christless world? So languid, so listless, and Pentecost just round the corner!

To us, as to them, the time of retreat brings memories. That is as it should be, provided always that we don't fritter away our time in empty day-dreaming. The graces God offered us, and the poor use we made of them; our sins, so far away in the past that the edge of contrition has been blunted, and yet seen, perhaps, in a truer perspective now that we have more experience of life; the shock of bad news, suddenly presenting us with a more serious view of the world; the sense of relief when some prayer that went long unheard was granted at last—all that makes a fitting background for our meditations. Only, if we are in a mood of discouragement, we find that these memories turn themselves into regrets. They only serve to remind us that we have changed and changed for the worse.

Changed for the worst at least to this extent, that we seem to have grown torpid and unresponsive; we have lost the elasticity we once had, the reserves of energy for good or evil. We seem to have gotten into a rut; we say our prayers without conviction, go about our daily work without enthusiasm, take our own imperfections for granted. Quite possibly we find less to mention, when Saturday night comes round, than we used to; we have learned to control our tempers rather better, find it rather less effort to heave ourselves out of bed in the morning—but is that anything really to record as progress? It all seems part of the rut; we cannot put our hearts even into those qualities of ours which pass for virtues. What is the use of going into retreat, when the horizon of our souls is bounded by such narrow limits? At best, it can only result in one or two resolutions that aim at merely mechanical improvement; I will cut down my smoking a little; I will go to bed at eleven—is this what we mean by taking on ourselves the yoke of Christ?

What I want to remind you of, at the very outset of this retreat, what it is enormously important you should always keep in mind, is that these times of flatness and discouragement are not the dreadful thing they seem. They won't be held against us, except in so far as we let ourselves be got down by them. All sorts of influences over which we have no control help to produce them, age and health and circumstances; there must be troughs as well as peaks in every human life—we are built that way. Please God, they will only be for us what they were for the apostles—a preparation for Pentecost. But what the devil is trying to do, what God is allowing the devil to do in order to test the genuineness of our purpose, is to make us despair of ourselves merely because we feel so second-rate. We're so convinced, always, that we can chart our own spiritual progress by watching the way we *feel* about religion; we expect divine grace to be something that produces a conscious glow of energy in us. We are like children, who won't believe that they've been given a present of money unless they can hear the coins jingling in their pockets. But of course divine grace isn't like that, mostly. Divine grace is like money paid into your bank, which never finds its way into your money-box.

Don't let us start our retreat, then, expecting too much of it; don't let's entertain exaggerated ideas about what it ought to be and do for us. There is no strong probability that, for you, it will be a sensational experience. It won't throw a flood of light on the way your life has been lived hitherto and represent in an equally clear light how it is that God wants you to behave instead. It won't bring tears of contrition to your eyes, or make you tremble at the thought of God's judgment, or make you long to die and go to heaven. It may be that nothing you hear, nothing you read in the course of it, will even pull you up short and force from you the silent admission "Good Lord, that's true." But if none of these things happens, don't be in a hurry to write down the retreat, and yourself, as a failure. Don't throw up the sponge and tell yourself that it's no use going on with the thing. On the other hand, don't force yourself into an attitude of dramatized contrition about being the kind of person you are, so hardened, so frivolous, so insensitive. These pious rhodomontades don't really help us on; three weeks from now you will have forgotten all about them. No, try to hold yourself steadily and humbly in the presence of God, telling him it's his will you should be making this effort, and there must be something he means his Holy Spirit to do in you; you are content to lie fallow and let the seed strike; you have no idea what it is, and very likely you never will. It may be, some phrase you have read here, quite unregarded at the time, will be stored up in some pocket of memory and come back to you later on—you will have forgotten the source of it and take it for an inspiration of your own. Be content to lie still in God's hands; only, do not refuse him anything—do not funk any train of thought for fear it should lead to uncomfortable consequences.

And, one other thing, "Together with Mary": try and put yourself in the position of those first apostles, who now and again, perhaps, in the course of their ungrateful novena, would steal a look at her motionless figure and wonder what thoughts were passing through her mind. Keep her close in view; the spring of her perpetual virginity will rejuvenate us. Come, Holy Spirit, not with outward manifestations, not with tongues of fire, but silently, as the warmth of spring creeps into the barren earth; come to this cenacle of a human heart and stir the dull airs of it with the breath of hope.

II

ALIVE TO GOD

In Matins of the Dead the words of the invitatory run: *Deum, cui omnia vivunt, venite adoremus*—"To God, all things are alive; O come, let us adore him".

All things, not all men; the body, which is dead to us, is still alive to God. Every particle of that dust is still obedient to his creative will; the same Power that once gave it freedom of movement is now exercised to imprison it in stillness; the same law which once ordained its growth now dooms it to decay. That, after all, is the astonishing fact: nothing can exist away from God; everything must, of necessity, come from him and tend to him. As the circle exists because each point on the circumference is in a particular relation to its centre, so the universe exists because everything in it is in a particular relation to God. As the satellites revolve round their planet, so everything in its creation keeps its place there by keeping its proper distance from God, who is its sphere. As the flowers open to the sun from which their vigor has returned to them, so in the natural and in the supernatural order all things turn continually towards God, who is their sun. All things are alive to God, react to him.

Do you doubt it? Then watch the actions of the Son of God, listen to the words of the Son of God, when he came to earth. You are crossing an inland sea in an open rowing-boat; suddenly, lashed by the draught that comes down through the funnel of those hills, the water rises about you in mountainous waves, tossing the boat from crest to crest, terrifying. They seem, those waves, to have all the greed and the fury of wild beasts; you have the illusion that the whole purpose of their ravening is to overwhelm this particular craft, in which you are voyaging—ah, if that were only so! Living beasts might be amenable to some trick of human mastery; these waves are senseless things; there is no art by which a human will can impose itself on them. But, wait a moment. One of your fellow-passengers rises from the bows of the boat, where he lay asleep, and looks out over those roaring billows as if they were a sea of children who had become too noisy over their play. With the tired but calm voice of a grown-up who knows how to deal with children, he says, "Peace, be still." And there is a dead hush instantly, a hush, almost, of expectancy, as if that noisy company were waiting to hear what game they should play next.

If Jesus Christ spoke on that occasion, it was for our sakes. He was thinking aloud, as a man will talk to some mechanical contrivance when he is explaining the nature of it to a set of pupils. The wind and the sea had no ears, to catch his human accents, nor any need of them. His will imposed itself directly on the forces of nature around him. You see, he was God. He said to the fig-tree, "Let no man eat fruit of thee henceforward", and it withered in a day. More curiously, when Saint Peter's mother-in-law was prostrated by fever, he did not say anything to her; he rebuked the fever, and it left her. On those special occasions, he put his thought into words but the same thing was happening, all the time. Everything was alive to him; it is hardly a metaphor, when Crashaw sums up for us the miracle at Cana of Galilee in the words "The shame-faced water saw its Lord, and blushed." Never a miracle but it demonstrates to us how faithfully and how readily material things obeyed him. Even the devils, though they came out reluctantly, came out at his command. It was only when he sought to impose his will on us human creatures that he encountered resistance. "Jerusalem, Jerusalem . . . how often I would have gathered thee. . . . Have I not chosen you twelve, and one of you is a devil?"

Let us remind ourselves of the obvious truth that the same thing is happening all over the world, and indeed in every corner of creation—a whole universe attentive at every moment to God's voice, at every moment alive to God, all of it except us, his children. Let us put it to ourselves more forcibly, by reminding ourselves that even *that* is only true where our conscious wills are concerned. Our bodies—they are alive to God all right. If you yawn in church, that may mean that your mind is not being attentive, but your body is being attentive to the divine will; each muscle reacts as God tells it to react. And I suppose the same is true, when you come to think of it, of our unconscious minds. If some memory intrudes itself upon your thoughts, a dangerous memory, which he allows to tempt you, a gracious memory, which he sends to inspire you, what exactly is happening inside you? This: that your unconscious memory, alive to God's voice, has been searching about in its lumber-room for the exact thing he wanted it to find. Only later, only when your *conscious* mind comes into play, does the temptation become a test at which you fail, the inspiration a grace with which you, somehow, do not correspond. Could anything be more humiliating to us than this spectacle of a listening universe in which we, and we only, are deaf to the divine call?

Saint Paul tells us that it ought to be otherwise; indeed (for he has a disconcerting trick of talking to us as if we already were what he wants us to be) Saint Paul tells us that it *is* otherwise. Partakers of the Resurrection, we must reckon ourselves "alive to God, through Jesus Christ our Lord". Alive to God—what do the words mean, when you apply them not to the body but to the soul, not to the unconscious but to the conscious mind? Go to the theologians, and they will tell you that every Christian soul is alive to God unless it is, at the moment, in a state of mortal sin. Yes, I suppose that's true. Let's paint for ourselves an imaginary portrait—please God, only imaginary—the portrait of a man who is *just* alive to God, and no more. It's some months now since he was at confession, but during that interval, more from the absence of temptation than from any fixed purpose of the will, he hasn't committed any mortal sin. He's been to Mass on Sundays, even put something in the plate; his children go to an excellent school, and he takes off his hat to the priest when he meets him. Beyond that, he doesn't do anything about it, and he doesn't mean to do anything about it. Pray? Why should he? Go into retreat? Oh dear, no. His last end? That'll have to look after itself. Charitable appeals? Well, there's always the waste-paper basket. Yes, quite true, he's not in mortal sin, and if he dies to-night I suppose we shall have to record that fact on his tombstone; it's difficult to see what other inscription we can devise. But—is such a man really *alive*?

I suppose what it all comes to is an ambiguity of phrase. Medically speaking, a man is alive even when he is dead drunk, or has been knocked senseless by an accident, or is in a coma. But when we send a boy on an errand and tell him to look alive, we don't mean him to look like a man in a coma. A prisoner in a concentration camp, deprived of all comforts, every means of amusing himself, still lives; but if we go to see him we don't ask whether he is enjoying life. No, in common speech we mean by "life" something more than mere respiration, mere circulation of the blood. We mean conscious, active life, throbbing in every vein, pulsing in every limb. And when we talk of the Christian life we mean, please God, something more than not being in mortal sin. We mean that a kind of spiritual vitality, however feeble, however fitful, is active in us and inspires us to act.

Saint Paul is always fond of using unexpected prepositions, and he is not content to tell us we ought to be spiritually alive; he says we ought to be alive to God. That, as we have seen, is plain common sense, because nothing can really be alive without being alive to God. But there is more than theology in it; there is psychology in it. A human being who is alive is alive *to* something, necessarily. At the lowest, I suppose it is possible to live to yourself. We do sometimes say, though heaven knows what right we have to pass any judgment of the kind, that we really believe So-and-so thinks of nothing but himself. Even that is a little more complicated than it sounds. Just reflect for a moment what it would mean, to think only of oneself—never to think about one's own qualities, or one's own exploits, or one's own grievances, only about oneself; never to think about the good dinner one was going to eat, or about the pleasant holiday one was going to have, only about oneself. The human mind couldn't stand it; we should go mad. No, the selfish person, the self-centred person, is not one who thinks about himself; he is one who thinks of everything, and of all other people, only in relation to himself. He concentrates his whole attention, as far as possible, on the things which minister to his own content, on the people who amuse or attract him. His ego, his dear old ego, is like the sun, which is not meant for looking at, but throws its light on all the things we do look at. The world, for him, is bathed in the sunlight of his own point of view.

That is the full-length portrait of the man who is alive only to himself. Of course, very few of us go through from the cradle to the grave living—if it can be called living—like that. Most of us have periods in our lives in which we are taken out of ourselves, as the saying is, and become alive to something else. A man falls in love; and for a little while, at any rate, somebody else instead of himself becomes the lantern which lights up the world for him, becomes the centre of reference which gives you the clue to his actions, and by which he interprets his experiences to himself. Or he becomes enthusiastic over a cause; it may be something quite tedious and insignificant, like vegetarianism or a fixed Easter, but it does for the time bring him to life a little, because he is not simply trying to live for himself. Once again, he is not thinking about the girl he is fond of the whole time, he is not thinking about a fixed Easter the whole time. His mind is occupied with a thousand things; but always this enthusiasm which has gripped him is there in the top-drawer, so to speak, of his unconscious mind; its influence bubbles up, overflows into his daily life, and makes it a life, at least, not utterly selfish.

Well, surely that is the sort of thing Saint Paul means when he tells us we ought to be alive to God: that God instead of self, God in preference to any other object of our desire or ambition, ought to be our centre of reference, ought to be the lantern that lights up the world for us. We can't be, directly, thinking about God all the time; even if we had the required powers of concentration, there would be daily duties which would interfere with the exercise. Your body, we saw just now, is attending to God (so to speak) the whole time; every slightest change that takes place in it is a direct reaction to his will. Your conscious mind cannot be attentive to God in that measure; it veers about, oscillates, is supple to a hundred influences.

For the matter of that, what we were saying just now about being wrapped up in yourself is equally true about being wrapped up in God, as really holy people are. The thought of God is not one which can satisfactorily occupy the central focus of the mind. When we try to think about him, our intellect beats about the bush, takes refuge in inferences and analogies; the thought itself escapes us. In so far as we try to make God the direct object of our attention we are always, aren't we, in reality trying to substitute an inferior image in place of him. We think of him as a King, but he doesn't really wear a gold crown; we think of him as up in the air, but he isn't really up in the air more than anywhere else. Being alive to God means something a little more complicated; it means that the thought of God is at the very apex of our unconscious minds all the time, overflowing all the time into our conscious thoughts, our conscious acts. It is like a taste in the mouth, a perfume in the nostrils, that conditions for the time being the whole of your experience, without your noticing that it is there. Not God in the very centre of the picture—that is not possible in this life, even for the saints—but God only just out of the very centre of the picture, so that he dominates the grouping of the whole. Alive to God, every thought of yours haunted—let us not be afraid to use that word for it—haunted by the divine presence.

I always like to illustrate that idea, at the risk of being undignified, by the attitude of a dog towards its master. An attitude which you may describe as one of habitual attention; the presence of its master makes all the difference, even when the dog is not, apparently, taking any notice of him. How curious it is, for example, that a dog doesn't really enjoy going for a walk without having a human being to accompany it! It will prowl round in a shifty sort of way, or go out hunting with another dog, but it will not go for a walk unless it is taken; it wants, you see, a centre of reference. It is preoccupied with its own canine interests, and yet all the time it is half thinking of its master; if it finds some treasure in the hedgerow, an old boot, for example, *that* must be brought out for its master's inspection and approval. If he kicks a stone, that stone is different from all the other stones in the road and must be carefully retrieved; if he whistles, how it pricks up its ears! Everything must be referred to him.

We read of the patriarch Enoch, that he walked with God. We usually, I think, get the wrong idea of that word "walked" in the Old Testament. We think of it as if it meant going on a kind of pilgrimage, laboriously plodding on and on, along a path that has been mapped out for you. But of course it doesn't; it means walking up and down, strolling about at your leisure, taking a turn up and down the front lawn—that is the sort of picture we want to have in our minds when we hear about people walking with God. Enoch walked to and fro, went about his daily business and his daily pleasures, but always with God.

If only we were more like that! If only we could walk through the world at God's heels—so close to him, so alive to his presence, that we could share everything with him, refer to him every moment of sunshine, every shadow of uncertainty in our lives; accept everything he sends with conscious gratitude; obey the least whisper of his call! Even if it is sitting in a room where its master is at work, see how the dog, though it is half asleep on the floor, is awake all the time to him; he has merely to throw a word to it, and you will hear it rapping its tail on the floor, for very pleasure that some notice has been taken of it—if we could be grateful, instinctively grateful, for every breath of grace that passes over our souls, and acknowledge it, at once, as God's gift!

How far we are, most of the time, even from that intermittent sense of God's presence! Even when we are doing something for him, how often we find that self, not God, is our true centre of reference! We take on some task with feelings of self-congratulation, because we are likely to do it well; we argue with a non-Catholic because we enjoy getting the best of an argument, enjoy putting our own view across, not consciously then and there wanting God's will to be done. Even when we are engaged in worshipping him, how often we think more of the people we are praying for than of the Person we are praying to, more of the ceremonies we are performing than of the King who is taking the march-past! Self always there, even when we are at our best; if only it were God always there, even when we are at our worst!

We would like to be alive to God, more than we are; can we do anything about it? Well, at least we can pray for it; it is a rare grace, but I do not think the request is presumptuous. I think, though, most of us could do something else, at least to predispose ourselves for the granting of such a favour. We could make a little more silence for God in our lives. We are so desperately keen, most of us, not to leave our attention unoccupied for a single moment: keeping the wireless on at all hours, picking up the newspaper, though we've already been through all that matters in it, just to while away three minutes before luncheon, humming a tune even as we walk down the street, as if we feared to be left, even for a moment, at the mercy of our thoughts—I wonder whether we couldn't afford, just now and again, to reverse that process? I mean to shut down, just for a minute or two, the busy distractions that are so welcome to us, and leave our minds free, by a deliberate interval of silence, to go back to God? They *will* go back to God, you know, if you let them; he is your centre, your sphere; there is no great effort of the mind needed, no fervent acts of the will. Just a minute or two stolen for God, when you find yourself waiting for a bus, or left with nothing to do while the kettle boils, or switching over from one occupation to another—I fancy this habit, cultivated for a little, would bring some of us nearer to the thing we want.

I wonder whether you are in the habit of making, now and again, a deliberate gesture of freedom? Throwing out both arms, as if to welcome the world to your embrace? Oh yes, I know it sounds rather like the gesture you make after a heavy meal or when you are feeling sleepy—"stretching yourself" our elders called it and discouraged the practice. In point of fact, there isn't much difference in the muscles you use; only this is a deliberate, not an instinctive gesture. When you regain the fresh air, after long hours of being cooped up in an examination-room; when the sun shines, some morning after a long spell of rainy weather; on the first day of your holiday—you make some such gesture as that as if to remind yourself, with gratitude, that you are alive. And it is that sort of gesture I am recommending to you, only this time it is a gesture of the supernatural life. You throw out your arms, as it were, towards Almighty God, reminding yourself that you are alive, alive to him, that you are awake and ready to listen.

III

TO-DAY

Saint Paul, in his epistle to the Hebrews, tells his fellow-countrymen, "Each day, while the word to-day has still a meaning, strengthen your own resolution." In obedience to that maxim, I want to give you a meditation on that single word "to-day".

Almighty God has given us, for the ordering of our lives, an alternation of day and night. "Each day echoes its secret to the next, each night passes on to the next its revelation of knowledge." The day by its brightness typifies his glory; the night by its darkness recalls to us the profundity of his mysterious being. And each day, as it were, waves its greeting to the last, bids us pick up our interrupted works, renew our plans, our hopes, our anxieties. Man goes forth to his work and to his labour until the evening; then night comes and with a kindly smile bids us put away all the toys we poor mortals make such a fuss over, shuts our books for us, hides our distractions from us, draws a great black coverlet over our lives. And so our life is marked out for us by alternations; each day is separated from the last by a thick black line of oblivion. Oh, we take up the burden of living where we left off; the griefs, the anxieties of yesterday return with the cold light of morning and dissipate the dreams which served for their anodyne. Still, it is something to have escaped their influence only for a few hours; we have gained some strength for the morrow. And meanwhile, this alternation of day and night has served another purpose; it stands to us for a model and a sacrament of human life in general. As the darkness closes round us, we go through a dress-rehearsal of death; soul and body say good-night to one another; and the soul wanders off into that unreal country where it can neither sin nor merit, can neither miss nor grasp opportunities. And then morning comes, and with morning, a re-birth.

Each day, then, begins with a birth and ends in a death; each day is a life in miniature. And the very conditions of our existence take away from us that excuse which is man's favourite excuse when he wants to shirk action and to neglect his salvation—that we do not know when to start. "Each day echoes its secret to the next"; yesterday whispers its word to to-day, and the word is "begin". For to-day is unique: it has never happened before; it can never happen again. For one moment it is all-important, fills the stage; to-morrow it will have taken its place among the unreal pageant of dead yesterdays. It has an importance, then, which is all its own; but this importance only belongs to it because it is one of a series. It may be the first of a series, the beginning of a new life. It may stand in the middle of a series, taking its colour from its fellows. And it may be the end of a series; it may be our last day on earth.

I want to think of it, in this meditation, under all those three aspects in turn. We may think of it as the beginning of a new departure. "To-day," says the Holy Spirit, "if you will hear his voice, do not harden your hearts." Yesterday and the day before you neglected it; but to-day is a fresh day, with a separate existence from the others; let it be the first of a fresh series of days, in which you will listen to the divine call. We may think of it as one day among others, with the same duties, cares, temptations as the others. "Deign, O Lord, to keep us, just for this one day, without sin." The day's evil is sufficient for it; if you will only preserve us from sin to-day, we can leave to-morrow to look after itself. Or we may think of it as the last of a series; one to-day will be the last of all our to-days; and it may be this. If to-day is to be the last, how are we to bear the thought of all our wasted yesterdays? Listen to our Lord speaking from his Cross, "To-day thou shalt be with me in Paradise"; it is never too late, for the Penitent Thief or for you and me.

First, then, we are to think of to-day as the beginning of a new series. I mean, O my God, to hear your voice to-day, not to neglect it as yesterday and the day before. There are, perhaps, words of yours which I have hitherto neglected or set aside, but not quite managed to forget; they still echo in my ears, like some human utterance which comes back to me after a little, although at the time I was not attending to it. Your voice has been suggesting to me that in this or that matter I might reform my habits; that I might serve you better by making this or that small sacrifice. And I heard the suggestion, and said to myself, "Oh, well, I can do that any day." Yes, but any day is no day; the only solution of the difficulty is "to-day". This is the day which the Lord has made—it was to-day you meant me to start. The long-refused invitation shall be accepted, at last.

Before we listen *to* the voice of God, we must listen *for* the voice of God; he speaks to us in a whisper, as he spoke to Elijah—we shall miss the sound if we do not make a silence to hear it in. When I say that, I don't want you to mistake my meaning. I don't think—this may be the most frightful heresy, but I don't think—that God very often puts things into your mind or mine when we are at prayer—inspirations, I mean, resolutions about what we ought to do for him. With the saints, evidently he does that; their prayer moves on an altogether higher level than ours. But the inspirations he sends to us are much more likely, I think, to come at other times of the day, when we aren't particularly attentive to him, or to the things of heaven. Nor do we realize at the moment that they are inspirations; we rationalize them, if I may talk the modern jargon, into quite ordinary dictates of common sense. Some little indulgence, perhaps, is spoiling our character by taking up too much of our time, or by claiming too much of our affections. Then quite suddenly one day, we say to ourselves, "Really, when one comes to think of it, such and such a thing is rather a waste of time. . . . Really I don't need quite so much of this or that as I've been in the habit of allowing myself." We think of it, you see, as an ordinary common-sense reflexion; really, it's God's voice talking to us. Only we must make a silence *in our lives* if God is going to talk to us like that. We must accustom ourselves to intimacy with him, to falling back on the thought of him at odd moments during the day, if these inspirations of his are going to pierce through to the summit of our consciousness. I dare say you don't find you want to make many resolutions in retreat; I never do make any resolutions when I am in retreat. Get back into the habit of recollection, and the resolutions will come to you afterwards, in disguise.

But of course that is not the only way in which God makes his voice heard. He does sometimes use exterior calls to throw a side-light on our lives. We may be reading some book, saying some prayer which we have said hundreds of times before, and suddenly there is a phrase which stands out from the page, which rouses an echo in our minds, as if it were meant for us; we feel, in the horrible phrase of the modern advertiser, "this means you". Or we may be struck with some good quality we see in the behaviour of a friend, and want to imitate it; or we may overhear a remark made about ourselves, or have it repeated to us, and suddenly become conscious of a defect in ourselves we never realized before. There are all sorts of ways of that kind in which God sends us his exterior calls; what we've got to do now is just to tell God that we will look out for them when they come and will not harden our hearts when they do.

Well, now let's think about to-day as one of a series, much like the others. Much like the others, and yet unique, it is picked out by the spotlight of the present. If you have read Père de Caussade's writings on spiritual abandonment, you will know what I mean when I talk about the sacrament of the present moment. Père de Caussade's is, I think, the most useful of all those shortcuts to perfection which spiritual authors have recommended to us. His point is that the job you are doing at the present moment, if it is your job, is quite certainly God's will for you; what you have to do is to throw yourself into that, abandoning your will to his over everything that will be and everything that might be, casting all your care on him, because he cares for you. You may be worried about what is going to happen to you and yours. The way for you to serve God is to focus all your attention on the job which is your job here and now, wearing blinkers, as it were, to hide from you the view of what you might be doing now, of what you may be doing later on. For to-day, our Lord tells us, to-day's troubles are enough.

And that applies, in a sense, even to our sins. After all, try as we will, there are some of our venial sins to which good resolutions seem to make no difference at all. The occasions of them are so frequent, the premeditation required for them is so small, that we cannot reach them at long range. We want to make a heroic resolve that we will never commit them again; but experience has taught us to distrust those resolves. Very well, then; here is a new use we may make of the magic word "to-day". Instead of worrying about whether we shall ever commit these sins again, let us simply resolve not to commit them to-day. "Deign, O Lord, to keep us, just for this one day, without sin"; let us see if we cannot cheat the devil, like some exacting creditor, by saying, "Not just yet; not to-day". And let us ask for no more than the grace to avoid those sins just in the sixteen hours which lie between bed-time and bed-time. Let us make to-day a holiday even from our venial sins. Even if we fall again to-morrow, something is gained.

This day without sin—as it is such a special day, we will try to avoid, his grace helping us, our sins against God, the little daily infidelities and irreverences by which we offend him. One day is very much like another, and for that reason it is terribly easy to get into a rut of imperfection—just a little longer in bed than will allow us full leisure to prepare for Mass and Communion, and so on all through the day, little bits of self-indulgence and self-pleasing. Deign, O Lord, this day to keep us from such sins against yourself.

This day without sin; as it is such a special day, we will try to avoid sinning against ourselves, by the wrong use of God's creatures. Walk out in the early morning and look at God's creatures; how beautiful they are, with the dew still clinging to them, and the new sunlight turning them all to silver, the flowers fresh as buds, the air pure, the birds singing as if they had never known what it was to sing before. (Saint Gertrude says that you ought to offer your heart to God every morning as a rose with the dew still on it.) In that early morning air, you recognize that every dawn is a re-birth; nature seems virgin, untarnished, only waiting for your sin, like a second fall of man, to rob it of its innocence. Well, to-day, as it is such a special day, we will try to keep that freshness and innocence of the morning all day in our hearts. We will not give in our names to that human conspiracy of sin which defaces God's creatures by misusing them. We will guard our eyes and all our senses, lest we should awake in ourselves that spirit of concupiscence which plays the serpent in this paradise of our nature. We will accept God's gifts of food and leisure and recreation lovingly and with grateful simplicity, yet careful not to let them get the better of us and interfere with our health or our usefulness.

This day without sin; as it is such a special day, we will try to avoid sinning against our neighbours. After all, we ought to know ourselves by now, and we ought to know our neighbours by now. We know almost exactly the people we shall be meeting to-day, their defects, their little weaknesses, their little jokes. We know the work we shall be having to do; perhaps we can make a fairly good guess at the food we shall have for dinner. We shall find ourselves talking to So-and-so, who will make us want to squash him; to So-and-so, who will tempt us to uncharitable conversation. But to-day is a holiday; we will put all that behind us. Deign, O Lord, to make this day a day unlike the others, a day without sin.

And then, for our third point, let us think of this new day as if it were going to be the last of all our days on earth. Let us imagine that you go to bed to-morrow night and wind up your watch just as usual; and letters are in the post, written to your friends, assuring them that you are quite well—and then, in the night, just a click in the mechanism of your body, a moment of horror in your dreams, and next morning the bell will be tolling for you, and your soul will have met its God in judgement. Can we find a text with the word "to-day" in it which will give us comfort and warning at the approach of death? Yes, we can remember our Lord's words to the Penitent Thief: "I promise thee, to-day thou shalt be with me in Paradise."

Cast your mind back to that familiar scene of our Lord's Crucifixion. Beside him stands a creature, the most beautiful that was ever formed since Adam lost his innocency.

In all her life no defiling thought has ever entered her being; there has been no action which was tainted with self, no moment at which her will was not perfectly united to the will of her Creator. Of such, you would say, is the kingdom of heaven. And on a cross, behind her, hangs a guilty wretch who is paying the last penalty for a career of crime. We have no evidence in Scripture that this man had ever harboured a generous sentiment, or possessed a redeeming virtue; even on the cross, his repentance is an afterthought. Of such, you would have said, the devil reaps his harvest of souls. Yet at the last moment, it may be, in which the gift of speech was granted him, he spoke a few words to his guiltless fellow-sufferer; and from that Heart, busy with all the tragedies of a universe, came to this one suppliant his sentence of reprieve: "Amen I say to thee, to-day thou shalt be with me in Paradise."

Yes, the Penitent Thief made an act of perfect contrition. He had done nothing to deserve such an opportunity, but he found, and he caught, the hour of grace. Mercy and pardon were all about him that day; here *is* the time of pardon; the day of salvation has come already. On that day of salvation he would harden his heart no longer. Not hell only, but Purgatory was baulked of its prey; he had gained the first plenary indulgence.

Let us hasten, then, while it is called to-day, to ask pardon with the Penitent Thief for our old sins. For we too, in times past, have lived only for the day; and the words "make the most of to-day, which now invite us to contrition", were once the motive of spiritual carelessness. We too, like those of whom the Wise Man wrote, have said, reasoning with ourselves, but not right, "Come, let us enjoy pleasure while pleasure is ours; youth does not last, and creation is at our call; of rich wine and spice take we our fill. Spring shall not cheat us of her blossoming, crown we our heads with roses ere they wither." And now all that is yesterday and is nothing; to-day is the reality, and that day our last this side of eternity. "I reflect upon days long past, the immemorial years possess my mind"; they are gone, those yesterdays, so brief, so fleeting, and nothing lies before us but an endless to-morrow.

And, as if that were not enough, there crowds in upon us, this last day, the memory of all we have left undone; all the inspirations which went unmarked, the calls which were left unheeded; all the opportunities we had, just for a moment, of doing some kindness to an unhappy fellow-creature, opportunities which were never repeated; all the time we wasted, frittered away on silly toys when we might have devoted its usefulness to God. "He has cut me off while the web was still in the making", we say with King Ezechias; we have looked for the rest of our years, and there was nothing left; "before the day reached its evening, he would make an end of me"—we are being cut off from life when we were only just beginning to live for God.

Here *is* the time of pardon; the day of salvation has come already; we can efface to-day, with salutary tears, the memory of those sins whose debt, to-morrow, we must needs expiate by suffering. Let us remember our sins each day, as if we had no more space left for sinning; let us weep over them, as if this were our last opportunity of contrition. And he, who returned to heaven with the Penitent Thief for his escort, will shorten our Purgatory and hasten to unite us with himself.

IV

THE FEAR OF DEATH

I hope you won't mind my prefacing my meditation on death by saying that I am only thinking aloud. In a sense, that ought to be true of all retreat meditations. They are far more likely to be useful if the preacher unfolds his own thoughts, trying to be honest with himself in the sight of God, than if he composes a series of edifying considerations which are suited—or so he imagines—to the needs of the people he is talking to. But it is especially so in this matter of death. Nothing is easier than to jot down, in a quite detached way, a set of copy-book phrases on the subject of death which have a very bold and defiant ring about them. But in fact the human animal differs enormously in its approach to this question; one of us is much more disposed than another to brood over it, one of us is much more disposed than another to take it calmly, one of us is much more eager than another to get quit of this life, so limited, so unsatisfactory, and face the immediate prospect of another world, however shadowy it may look. What I am giving here is my own reactions to the subject of death. And what I say will probably be of use only to people who happen to be constituted more or less as I am.

For most of us, I think, the meditation on death is an effort; we have to set our teeth and go through with it. I suppose that, as we live casually from day to day, we are all the time unconsciously repressing (perhaps even consciously repressing) the unpalatable thought. Just as you will sometimes find yourself ignoring the existence of a person you greatly dislike—some public man, for instance, whose writings or utterances annoy you, so that the mention of his name gives you a sudden feeling of irritation, merely by reminding you that there is such a person—so it is with this common enemy of our race we call death; unconsciously, we try to cheat ourselves into the belief that he is not there, although we know he is. A small girl I know was asked by her mother what she would say if God told her that he wanted her to be a martyr. And she replied without a moment's hesitation, "I should say, 'What?'" How well one knows that habit among children of saying "What?" when they have heard perfectly well what you said, and are only trying to stave off the question, get rid of it somehow. And so it is with many of us grown-up people; when God whispers in our ear the warning that one day, perhaps soon, we must die, our instinct is to say "What?" and hope that he won't raise the subject again.

There is no reason why we should be desperately ashamed of ourselves when we find that we want to do that. Because, after all, in a sense death is something which is not natural to us. Oh, I know that the immortality which Adam and Eve would have enjoyed if they had not fallen did not really *belong* to them, was not something owed to the completeness of their nature; it was a special gift of God which God had the full right to take away from them. But for all that, soul and body are made for one another, and when our bodies lie in the dust and our souls have to exist in Purgatory in a disembodied state, it is a *kind* of violation of the natural order. From that disorderliness we shrink, not merely with the physical instinct of animals that struggle against the immediate onset of mortality, but with a long-distance feeling of resentment. That is an instinctive reaction of ours, that feeling that we are being somehow defrauded when life is taken away from us. Obviously it is not an attitude which we consciously adopt; it would be an irreverent and unreasonable attitude to adopt—irreverent because it assumes that we, God's creatures, have rights against him; unreasonable from every point of view. If man is made for eternity, and this life is only a preface, though a very important preface, to another life in another world, then it is fitting that we should think of ourselves, here and now, as soldiers on sentry duty, ready to be relieved by our Commanding Officer at a time of his own choosing. It keeps us up to the mark, not knowing when we shall be called to account. It makes us work harder, serving God and helping our fellow-men, if we know that our opportunities are strictly limited; "it may be", we say to ourselves, "that I shall not pass this way again", and we hasten to do some act of kindness, because we may never have such another opportunity. The thought of death is good for us, too, because it prevents us getting too much wrapped up in this world, and the goods of this world; shrouds have no pockets. Oh yes, all the copy-book considerations are quite unanswerable, if we try to argue that death is a kind of injustice on God's part. But all that doesn't stifle the instinct in us which makes us want to go on living. We are born for immortality, and although our faith tells us that death is not extinction, it is much too like extinction to let us feel comfortable about it.

Perhaps we try to console ourselves with the reflexion that life gets more and more unpleasant as it goes on, and therefore when it comes to the point it won't much matter. How dreadful, the gradual failure of one's powers, the childish weakness of body, sometimes of mind! How dreadful the long months of pain that may precede death, the drastic efforts of the doctors to prolong life, the vista of bottles on the table over there in the corner! If death comes to us, quite soon, quite suddenly, at least it means we shall miss all that. If we live on, to go through all that, at least by the time we have gone through it we shall feel ready for death—we shall have gotten tired of waiting about in its antechamber. So we tell ourselves; but does it really help much? Rather, I think, the effect of brooding over those bottles is to magnify the stature of death in our own minds, make us shy at it still more. How formidable an enemy, which can thus cast its shadow before it! And can we really believe that death is only the gate to immortality, when we see, or think of, a human body being taken to pieces bit by bit, first one faculty deserting it and then another?

People with lively imaginations who feel like that about death ought not, I fancy, to meditate on it, at least in the strict sense of the word "meditation". Let them meditate on the shortness of life; let them meditate on hell, or on Purgatory. But to feast their terrors by deliberately reconstructing the picture of a death-bed or of a graveyard will be a waste of time, I think, if not worse. The meditation on death is meant to be an expedient for turning libertines into Jesuits by frightening them; with the best acts of will in the world, it is not calculated to embolden the timid.

But (it may be very properly argued) although the meditation on death is not well suited to certain temperaments, surely each of us, however constitutionally nervous about death, ought to have a prayer-attitude on the subject? Surely it ought not to be a thing we have to tuck away and forget about when we approach God, this transition from a world of shadows to a world of realities, this carriage he graciously sends to fetch us, when he wants us to come and join him? And indeed, there is a scruple—perhaps it is something more than a scruple—which often assails us if we find that the thought of death does not fit in easily into our prayer. "Can it be", we ask ourselves, "that I really haven't got any faith? That I go on saying, day after day, *I believe in the resurrection of the flesh, and the life of the world to come*, but it's only a formula to me; I don't really *believe*?" If we really had faith, could we hesitate, for a moment, about the act of crossing the threshold from time into eternity?

That's a question which forces itself on you, I think, if you read John Wesley's journal. Here you have a man whose whole life is centred on God, who spends the whole day, methodically arranged, in a long round of worshipping God and doing good, an ascetic, who treats himself very hardly, a charitable man, who goes round visiting prisoners in jail; and yet he is afraid of death. The sight of some German fellow-passengers, members of the obscure Moravian sect, who sing hymns with apparent unconcern when everybody on board believes the ship is just about to founder in a storm, pulls him up and makes him wonder whether he is a Christian after all. He goes through an experience of "conversion", and for the rest of his long career he looks forward to death without a tremor and teaches innumerable other souls to do the same. Nothing encourages him so much as the sight of criminals who have come under his influence going to the gallows in the joyful assurance of a happy eternity. Nothing, it must be added, disedifies him so much as the Irish agitators he meets, condemned to execution, who break down on the scaffold although they have received the last ministrations of the Catholic Church.

And yet you can point to pious Anglicans, like his contemporary and friend Dr. Johnson, who went in fear of death all their lives. When Boswell tried to draw him on the subject of death, the great man lost his temper and insisted on changing the subject. What was it exactly that Wesley had, and Johnson hadn't? Curiously, I think you may say it was something quite, quite unimportant. Wesley had gotten hold of an ecstatic type of religion, Protestant rather than Catholic, which fixes firmly on the emotions, dominates the imagination, and makes the things of eternity seem real to a man, as if they lay within the range of his ordinary experience. Johnson was content, as most of us have to be content, with beliefs accepted on hearsay, proposed to him by the Church to which he belonged, and accepted with a firm direction of the will and intellect. I doubt if Johnson had less faith (in the more general sense) than Wesley; it is possible to argue that he had more. It is possible to argue that the true business of faith is not to produce emotional conviction in us, but to teach us to do without it.

To do without it—here at last I believe we have hit upon some comfort of the unheroically minded. Is it possible that the hall-mark of the true Christian is not, necessarily at least, being brave about death, but rather, being prepared to offer whatever shrinking he feels about it as part of the sacrifice which he makes of his life to God? Fear is not a sin. You may sin through fear, by neglecting your duty, by denying your faith, granted. But fear in itself is not a sin—or what was our Lord doing in Gethsemani? It seems to me that whatever were the precise feelings which there assailed him—in our Latin version, they are feelings of fear and disgust; the Greek is perhaps better represented if we say that he began to be mystified and dismayed—he was evidently condescending, as far as Incarnate God could, to our human weakness, and inviting us to unite our secret misgivings about death with the sacrifice he was making then. We were to see—that is how I read the story—that we should not be held responsible for having a dry feeling in the mouth, and a quaking about the legs, in moments of danger; that was not the point. The point was, first, that we should do our duty, whatever inward tremors we had to crush down in the doing of it. And second, that we should make an offering to God of this human weakness, this shameful disability, and tell him, "My God, I know I'm a coward, but

I want to offer my terrors, like every other discomfort my human destiny involves, to you. Cowards die many times before their deaths; and *all* those deaths I offer to you."

I think one of the best of Monsignor Benson's books is *The Coward*. The hero of that book, if hero is not the wrong name for it, is discredited in the eyes of his father and his family by showing fear on one or two critical occasions. Then, at the end of the book, a fire breaks out, and he rushes into a burning house to save something—I forget what. Trapped there, he appears at a window, gibbering with fear, and then is overpowered by the smoke. Was he a coward? Or was the act which cost him his life all the more meritorious because it demanded a greater moral effort in him to do it, than it would have in what we call a brave man? *The Imitation of Christ*, which always has the last word on every subject, reminds us that what God takes into account is not so much the things we do as the apparatus we have, to start with, for doing them.

Is that all, then—ought death to come into our prayers simply as one of the things which some of us are afraid of (like spiders), things which can be "offered up"? Are we never to pray about what our death is going to be like—apart, of course, from asking God to give us the grace of perseverance? I remember the late Archbishop Goodier, who gave me my ordination retreat, saying this; that it was a good thing to pray for the kind of death that appealed to you. It was surprising, he said, how often you found that particular prayer granted. I have wondered since whether Archbishop Goodier, who was an extremely holy man, prayed that he might have a sudden death, because he didn't like the idea of the bottles. A priest went to call on him one day down at Teignmouth, and the Archbishop saw him off at the door. When he got a little way away, he saw the door still standing open; so he went back and found the

Archbishop just inside, dead. Another of these holy men, the late Abbot of Buckfast, had a great horror of death; and he, after spending a day or two in bed with a bit of a cold, told the infirmarian he would be getting up next day; there was no excuse for treating himself as an invalid any longer; and he was found dead in the morning.

Meanwhile, if we stand back from the portrait of death, cease to view it in all its ghastly detail and try to take in the general significance of the picture, there's something more to be said about it, and something which is of the first consequence for our prayers. The point to seize on is surely this: that birth and death are the best possible reminder of our creatureliness. We creatures are, and God is not, in time. We find ourselves in a hurry; this creature of time, which does not enter at all into God's existence, conditions our lives and makes all the difference to us. We find ourselves bored with waiting; this creature of time, which does not enter at all into God's existence, can become a kind of martyrdom to us. The two moments, then, of birth and death, the moment when we step onto, and the moment when we step off, this shifting platform of time which is our world, are essentially moments of consecration. With the first, we had nothing to do. When the second comes, we do not know whether we shall be in a posture to devote it, by a conscious act, to the glory of God; it may be very sudden. it may come (it does very often) when we are unconscious. We want, then, especially in time of retreat, to make a preliminary offering of it into God's hands.

Your whole life should be a sacrifice offered to God in union with our Lord's sacrifice in the holy Mass. The crucial moment in the holy Mass is when the priest says, *Hoc est Corpus meum*. And in our sacrifice the crucial moment is that of death, when we too say, *Hoc est corpus meum*. "This is my body, Lord, the body thou gavest me, and art now taking away from me, the body in which I have suffered, and sinned. Come, holy oils, and seal these gateways of sense, the points of contact in me between body and soul; seal them well, this is a secret present from me to my God." And if death is the moment of consecration, we, as we look forward to it now, are making our offertory; we are holding out our bodies on the paten, ready against the moment when they will be caught away from us in the consummation of the sacrifice. In a fallen world, sacrifice means the destruction, the annihilation, as far as possible, of the thing offered. It is God's merciful decree that death should not be a complete annihilation. But this separating of soul and body is the nearest thing to annihilation which it is ours to give. Let us look forward, then, to death, as the moment at which we shall make to God the supreme confession of our creatureliness, when we shall immolate, in honour of his eternity, this transitory existence of ours, offer him this candle, to be blown out. The dearer a thing life seems to you, the harder it seems to relinquish, the more motive for generosity in offering it. So little, the real value of the sacrifice we make, when we give our souls into his hands; all the better, then, if (by a kind of sentimental value) it means much to us, who make it.

V

WATCHING

It is curious how often, in reading the Bible, you come across some resemblance, some echo, some pair of companion pictures here and there, which makes you draw breath as at a discovery. The thing seems to stick out a mile, and yet the sacred authors give no sign that they were conscious of it—can it have been a mere coincidence? Surely not. Surely Divine Providence arranged that things should fall out just as they did, precisely in order to let you and me trace a pattern in sacred history, and, finding that pattern so evidently there, make bold to guess that there is a pattern in our own lives too.

One such pair of companion pictures must have often arrested our attention in the Gospels, I mean, our Lord lying asleep during the storm on the Lake, and our Lord's apostles falling asleep in Gethsemani. No need to draw out in detail the poignancy of either situation. "Master, art thou unconcerned? We are sinking!" It is on his errand that they have undertaken the perilous journey; it is in his service that they struggle so manfully with oar and tiller; and he? The winds howl, the waves roar, but they do not wake him; God sleeps, while man watches. "Simon, art thou sleeping? Hadst thou not strength to watch even for an hour?" Here is a man singled out, with two of his fellows, to witness the agony of God, to comfort, for one hour, the restlessness of the Eternal. There is no time to be lost; vigilant enemies are on their way, and the opportunity will never be repeated. And he? He drops off to sleep, as if it were you or I. God watches, while man sleeps.

It is a rhetorical convention in the Old Testament, in the Psalms especially, to complain that Almighty God has gone to sleep, to bid him awake and take cognisance of what is going on in the world—his world, providentially ordered. Here was a nation singled out among all the other nations, betrothed to the Creator of the world by an eternal covenant, his own people. The country in which it dwelt was his cherished possession; on the slopes of Mount Sion rose the Temple in which somehow, mysteriously, he dwelt. And yet it was only for a few years, nine centuries before Christ, in the reign of King Solomon, that this most favoured nation took rank as a world-power. At all the other periods of its history you see it at the mercy of its more powerful neighbours; Assyrian, Babylonian, Persian, Greek, and Roman armies sweep over it by turns—a history of inglorious vassalage and impotent revolt. What was God doing all the time? Could he really be asleep, that he should take no notice? Or could it be that he was only, so to say, shamming sleep, that he was waiting for the moment when heathen arrogance had reached its full extent, and then, suddenly, the day of his vengeance would dawn? The Christ would come and set up a world-empire of peace and justice, with Jerusalem for its centre, the Jewish people for its governing caste!

The Christ came and brought them a message of disappointment. The more closely you read our Lord's early parables, the more clearly you read one message in them. His kingdom on earth is not going to be a world-empire of peace and justice at all. The world will go on as it always has; it will be a ding-dong struggle between the powers of light and the powers of darkness; there will be tares mixed up with the wheat, now as before. It will still look as if God were asleep; not till the final judgement shall we know that he was watching all the time. And that scene on the Lake of Galilee was, surely, a kind of acted parable, expressive of all this. Our Lord wanted us to see that storm-tossed boat as the image of his Church—wanted us to see that it is precisely the people who are running his errands, doing his work, that must expect to have the roughest passage. All down the centuries, it will look as if God were asleep; and we, in our little faith, shall be crying out, "Master, art thou unconcerned? We are sinking!" There will be no sign, but God will be watching, just as our Lord himself, sleeping in the bows of the boat, nevertheless (can we doubt it?) knew what was happening. He will awake at a moment of his own choosing, and the world will come to an end suddenly, like an evil dream.

In his later parables, our Lord seems to change both the symbolism and the emphasis. Almighty God is represented not as a man who goes to sleep, but as a man who goes off on a journey to some far-off country, leaving his servants behind him on their good behaviour. The change of symbolism does not matter much; evidently the man who goes off on a journey, like the man who falls asleep, is in no position, here and now, to interfere; it is God's apparent neglect of his creation that is thrown into relief. But the change of emphasis is more important; our Lord is no longer concerned to arm us against despair; he is warning us against negligence. Because God seems to take no notice, man is tempted to take no notice either. Why be at pains to observe God's law in the strict letter of it, when so many people in this wicked world openly flout both the letter and the spirit of it, and nothing happens to them? The problem is as old as the Old Testament, but it would be idle to pretend that it has no influence on people's minds in our own day. They do not say it openly, but they feel the tug of the temptation. Unprovided death? Well, they will take their chances of that. And our Lord's answer is, "What I say to you, I say to all, Watch."

As if another acted parable were needed to drive that lesson home, he chose, knowing what would come of it, his little body-guard for Gethsemani. God's special servants, the rulers of his Church, how terrible is their need of vigilance! The prophet Ezekiel was told that he stood in the position of a watchman, posted on a vantage-point so as to warn his people of the remotest threat of danger on the horizon; if he failed in his duty, he would be held to account for it. And here they are, Peter and James and John, posted as sentries among the olive-trees; it will be good practice for them. There is a kind of dreadful irony in the situation; the householder in the parable, if you remember, went off to a very far country, and our Lord goes off, how far? Just a stone's throw away. But all three fall asleep at their posts. "My Father, if it be possible"—what is not possible, after this?

Paradox was part of our Lord's teaching method. He would underline the moral he wanted to convey by throwing what he had to say into an almost exaggerated form, regardless of inferences. How was he to explain to us the importance of being unwearied in prayer? He would tell us the story of a widow who was trying to gain redress from a corrupt judge, and only succeeded at last by sheer importunity. What did it matter representing his heavenly Father, for the purposes of the story, as a corrupt Judge? The theologians would put that all right afterwards. And so it was, when he was explaining to us the importance of being always on the watch, always at full tension. Do you remember what he says? "Be sure of this; if the master of the house had known at what time the thief was coming, he would have kept watch, and not allowed his house to be broken open." Almighty God a thief! Yes, that is the picture he invites us to contemplate, when we are meditating on watchfulness: the householder leaning out of the front window and nervously scanning the patch of grass where the lamp-light falls; "there doesn't *seem* to be anyone about; surely it would be safe to go to bed?" And there, in the bushes, is the thief dancing with impatience, waiting for the moment when the light will go out and the family will be at his mercy. If only thieves kept a time-schedule, how much lighter we should sleep! If only Almighty God's visitations were less sudden, what an invitation to all of us to live carelessly!

At least—would it be? I think we all feel that this idea of watchfulness as a mere determination not to be caught napping is rather a low standard to set before ourselves. It reminds us uncomfortably, perhaps, of our school-days, when the amount of work we did, and the amount of time we spent in kicking our neighbour's shins, depended very much on whether the master was or wasn't watching—at least, on whether we thought he was or not. Perhaps in those days—I think it's rather liable to happen with schoolboys—we did dwell too much on the idea of God watching us, and the idea that it was necessary for us to be on the look-out accordingly. We had seen old-fashioned churches, perhaps, in which there was a representation, over the chancel arch, of an enormous Eye, the wakeful Eye that was looking at us all the time, sizing us up all the time. We had seen lodging-house bedrooms in which the illustrated text was prominently displayed, "Thou, God, seest me". And it encouraged us to think of Almighty God under the image of a superhuman policeman, who was always in wait for us just round the corner. In proportion as we felt like that, we were in danger of growing up in a scrupulous habit of mind, or perhaps, in the carelessness of youth, becoming reckless, and exorcising the distasteful idea from our minds, with lamentable results. Surely this is one of the childish ways we ought to outgrow when we reach manhood? Surely this is to be governed by fear; and Saint Paul tells us that we ought no longer to be governed by fear, now that God has sent his Spirit into our hearts and encourages us to pray to him as our Father!

I think that's probably true. I think, as I was saying just now, that our Lord deliberately heightened the colours of the pictures he drew for us—deliberately threw into relief the main point he was getting at, without meaning us to make difficulties about the details. In the parable of the Unjust Judge he was only showing us how important it is to go on praying, and in this remark of his about the thief in the night he is only showing us how important it is not to let our attention stray from the great business of the Christian calling. He does not mean us to think of watching as a purely negative thing; to watch is not merely to refrain from sleep, out of fear that some uncomfortable thing may come along, and we shall be caught napping. To watch has a positive implication; it means being on the tip-toe of expectation; it means craning your neck out of the window in the hope that you will be the first to cry out, "Look! They're coming!" And that, I suppose, is why our Lord gives us almost in the same breath a much more gracious image of his return. He tells his disciples that they must be "like men awaiting their master's return from a wedding feast, so that they may open to him at once when he comes and knocks at the door. Blessed are those servants, whom their master will find watching when he comes; I promise you, he will gird himself, and make them sit down to meat, and minister to them." I don't think that is meant to be a merely fanciful description. I think we are meant to understand that the master, when he left the wedding-feast, has begged a few snacks to take with him, a roast here, a bottle of wine there, "just for the people at home, you know". And he signalizes his home-coming by sharing out the wedding dainties: "Here, it's your turn now; sit down and have your fling." Has anybody drawn for us a more comforting picture of heaven than that?

Saint Peter, as always—it is a gift of his—asks the question we were wanting to ask: "Dost thou address this parable to us, or to all men?" Is it only the apostles, wearied out with all the labours which Saint Paul describes; is it only their successors, the shepherds who keep watch over his flock, that our Lord invites so consolingly? Or does it hold out hopes to the common ruck of people, to you and me? Our Lord's answer isn't a direct one, but it tells us all we want to know. He merely says that the more important you are, the more severely you will be punished, if you fail in your duty. Not difficult, though, to see that on the same principle there will be a gradation of rewards; and if so, not all rewards are for the heroes. You and I, in our small way, are servants awaiting our Lord's return—just peeping over the edge of the banisters, but waiting for a smile to be thrown to us too.

Only—let us be clear about it—that doesn't mean sitting about with folded hands waiting for the Last Judgement to come and telling one another how disordered the world is. However disordered the world is, you and I are meant to *watch* in the positive sense; we are meant to tidy things up, as well as they can be tidied up, against the day of our Lord's return—like servants waiting for their master's homecoming, not anticipating it with alarm, and deciding that it will be better not to have a dance in the drawing-room for fear he should come back in the middle—No, looking forward to it, running out on to the drive to see if they can catch the sound of carriage-wheels. And, in the intervals of that, doing a hundred little odd jobs *against time*; always a room to be dusted here, a floor to be polished there, a fire to be made up there, so that the house will look a hundred percent comfortable when he steps inside. Each of us has got a job to do; each of us should be inspired to do it better if it looks as if we hadn't got much time to do it in.

It takes different people different ways. Some people get so interested in their work that they become parochial and narrow-minded—cannot see beyond the edge of their own cabbage-patch. The world passes them by; they are never thrilled by the vicissitudes in human affairs. Other people think in continents and are depressed, nowadays, by the exercise; reading the morning paper is enough to put them off work for the rest of the day; what is the use (they object) when everything is going from bad to worse? But the Christian ought to rise above both these temptations. The business of his soul, his daily work, his common human duties are, to him, a charge entrusted to him; with Père de Caussade, he believes in the sacrament of the present moment; what might happen, what is likely to happen, he leaves in the hands of God. He does not forget, in his prayer, the perils of the Church, the needs of suffering humanity everywhere. But he knows that God is watching too. Watching, not merely in the negative sense of waiting and doing nothing, so as to catch his enemies, at last, red-handed, but in the sense of caring for the destinies of his own servants; he, watching over Israel, slumbers not nor sleeps. World events, somehow, fit into an arranged pattern; all is foreseen; all is provided against. With that confidence, and with the confidence that he, too, has a tiny part to play in the shaping of that pattern, the Christian goes about his daily work with unremitting energy. He is a sentry at his post, with divine orders to be on the watch.

Is that all that is meant by "watching"? In the first days of Christianity, it's pretty clear that our Lord's command to watch was interpreted in a quite literal sense. Saint Paul tells the Colossians to persevere in prayer and keep watchful over it, and we know that at Troas the Christians met for prayer late at night; the whole idea of vigils, which is embedded in the liturgy, shows what the practice of earlier ages was. Many of the saints are praised for their habit of spending whole hours in this way; Saint Patrick, you will remember, got through the whole psalter every night. Nowadays, there is no survival of all that, except in the midnight Mass of Christmas Day and now of Easter. The hymn at Matins, all through Lent, mentions sleep as one of the things we have got to ration for the occasion. How is it that we have gotten out of the habit of really keeping vigil? And, in these times when we are being called upon to do special acts of penance, mightn't it be appropriate if we revived the practice?

Usually, when we stay up late to say our prayers, it means that we have been playing bridge all the evening, and perhaps it would have been better to sacrifice the bridge than the sleep. But I confess that even if you have done a full day's work, such a full day that there was no time to get your prayers in, I should be very reluctant to counsel sitting up at night over them, where they are not actually of obligation. It's not that one yawns over one's prayers, or goes to sleep in the middle; our Lord doesn't mind that—he remembers Gethsemani. But it means you will be yawning next day, just when you are trying to look interested; it means you will be snappish and disposed to nag at people; and in the long run you are making demands on your nervous health, in times when most of us want all the nervous health we have got. No, I think we shall do better to leave that to the religious, and try to do our best with less heroic remedies, such as getting up when we are called, and going to bed when we say we are going to—to be on the watch; to shake off, not weariness of the body, but lethargy of the mind. It won't matter frightfully if the Day of Judgement comes and finds us asleep in bed. What *will* matter is if it finds us sitting about in arm-chairs and telling one another that the world isn't worth saving.

VI

THE WORLD TO COME

It is a traditional feature of a retreat, to reinforce its lessons about sin and carelessness by drawing attention to the punishments which await us after death if we play with the divine mercy. If I attempt something of this sort, let me plead my own want of the artist's imagination as my excuse for not portraying those punishments in lurid colours. The consciousness, too, that when you are doing that you are indulging in metaphor, that you are translating things of which we have no experience into terms of flesh and blood, makes it a more difficult task. I want to approach the subject from a different angle. I would ask you to think of your own human feelings, your own human reactions to the sort of distressing situations with which we are all familiar, and get some notion of what punishment must be like in a future life by magnifying those feelings to scale. After all, that is what happens when somebody tries to describe to us a poignant experience which is altogether outside our own range—if a soldier, for example, is trying to describe to us what it is like advancing in face of the enemy. Almost at once you will find him taking refuge in the formula "I felt as if" so-and-so. Our feelings, after all, are the obvious link between the life we lead here and the life we shall be leading when we come face-to-face with eternity.

Very few people, I imagine, feel sure that they are going to hell. Those who die in the faith, but without charity, mostly think, wouldn't you say, that they are all right, they have just scraped through. And those who have lost the faith, or who die in sin outside the influence of the faith, probably lay some flattering unction to their souls—it will be all right, they think, they will be given another chance. Up to the moment when they are taken away, this world of creatures treats them no more unkindly than any soul predestined to eternal life. The sun gives them its warmth; they are fed and clothed and housed; the scent of flowers is theirs to enjoy, and music, and the bright colours of spring; the resources of civilization are at their disposal; the railway carries them about like anybody else; the post brings up their letters like anybody else's. So perfect is the illusion of security all around them, that they forget God, and forget they are forgetting him. I don't mean to say that, in many cases, they lose belief in his existence; probably if you could really look into their hearts, and get behind the mask they wear, most of them still believe in God; but they forget about him, and go on making use of his creatures all the same. They are like people heavily in debt, who somehow contrive to go on and on incurring fresh debts, knowing all the time, really, that they are on the high road to ruin, but somehow contriving to shelve the ugly consideration and rid their minds of it. We can, you see, do that to God; he allows us to forget about him, if we insist on it. To the last, even when the shadows darken round the death-bed, the conspiracy of illusion is there; perhaps the last sensation which people in that position experience is that of the holy oils closing their eyes and ears and lips, just like those of any other Christian person. But there has been no repentance, and the holy oils have no power to accomplish their charitable office.

And then, quite suddenly, the bottom falls out of that world. On this side, the approach of death, the failing of the senses, has been gradual; on the other side, there is no gradual awakening, as if from a dream. The soul wakes up all in a moment into a world of realities, and knows, in that moment, that it is lost. True, it is judged; but the tribunal of that other world knows nothing of the slow processes of law; "the man who does not believe", we read in Saint John, "is condemned already"; a crisis has taken place, and it is all over. The man has woken up from a world full of material creatures, where God was forgotten, into a world from which all material creatures have slipped away, and there is nothing to think about except God.

God, who gave that material world he has come from all its reality, is now the only reality left; and with a great hunger of loneliness the heart that was made for him turns back to him—and God is not there. The sinful soul has created for itself, as it were, a godless universe. The soul cannot do without God any longer; creatures vanish from its grasp; it is thrown back on its need for God, and God is not there. And now, seeing things for the first time in the light of eternity, it feels at the same moment an unspeakable craving for eternal happiness, and a consciousness that that craving must remain for ever unsatisfied. It's as if a person playing blind-man's-buff had suddenly torn off the bandage, only to realize that he was blind—ah, what a feeble image! Man can live without light. But the soul in eternity without God has lost the whole element in which alone it can live. True, the unseen power of God maintains it in existence; it exists, but it does not live. It is like a clock without hands; it has lost its whole reason for existing. That sense of confusion, of being unforgivably angry with oneself, which we have all felt before now on so many trivial and inappropriate occasions, finds its full scope now, and that posture of the soul is eternal. For all eternity, that man is his own enemy.

Do you know what it is to start the day in a thoroughly bad temper, put out of humour by some misadventure at the beginning of it? You have missed an important train, perhaps, or you have gotten into a temper unreasonably, and it has ruffled you, a bad omen to begin your day's work with. Unless you have unusually steady nerves, you will know the effect of such an experience on your peace of mind, how you find fresh food for disgust in everything you come across. Each little petty annoyance, knocking your head against something or sitting in a draught or having somebody next you who whistles to himself, becomes so intolerable an annoyance that you feel you want to scream with rage. Why is that? Because you are not at peace in yourself; and to the man who is not at peace in himself there can be no peace in his surroundings either; the world is at war with him. Now, if you multiply that experience to the scale of eternity you will catch some glimpse of what hell must be like. The sufferings of sense are only the echo, as it were, of that deep-rooted discomfort which pervades our whole being. As we saw, so long as his earthly life lasted the unhappy man could call upon the creatures around him for their services like the rest of us, and they obeyed him. There was nothing to warn him that he was an outlaw in God's universe. But now, now it is all different. A soul made for God, which finds itself in eternity cut off from God, is a complete misfit; we are at war with ourselves, and therefore our whole environment is at war with us. We cannot, with our limited imaginations, form any very accurate picture about what our environment will be like in a future existence. But we can be quite certain that, to the lost soul, that environment will be utterly hostile. Put it in this way: if a lost soul entered heaven by mistake, the music of heaven would seem to it like a series of hideous discords. It carries the seeds of its own misery in itself.

I don't mean to suggest that the pain of sense which is experienced by the lost souls is merely a consequence of that other punishment of theirs, the pain of loss. The pain of loss will be felt equally, it is to be supposed, by all alike; the pain of sense will, according to the common opinion, be graded so as to suit the various degrees of guilt. No, what I am trying to put to you, though of course it is only guess-work, is that the pain of sense will reverberate in the lacerated feelings of the lost soul till both pains become one; the pride which rejects punishment will make the punishment itself more difficult to endure; the lost soul will be a focus of impotent rebellion against the whole order of things in which it finds itself. Just as the man whose nerves are thoroughly on edge cannot tell you for certain whether his annoyances come from within or from without, so that intense dis-ease which the lost soul experiences is neither wholly from within nor wholly from without. It is the reaction of a nature out of sympathy with the whole order of things around it; like a cracked bell, it must go on giving out a false echo to every blow that is struck on it.

Think of a tyrant, walking about on the eve of a revolution that is to hurl him from his throne. Everyone about him obeys his slightest whim; there are cheers in the streets as he passes through; he can command any luxury he wills. To-morrow, he will be slinking about as a fugitive, every man's hand against him, the whole of society his enemy. That is the true portrait of the man who goes about this world careless of his eternal destiny. All God's gifts are still at his service; he is surrounded everywhere by the beneficence which attends us human creatures; nature smiles on him. If he dies to-night, all that will be changed. It is not merely that the God he has forgotten will be his Judge. The whole order of things in which he lives will have become his enemy; beauty and kindliness will have dropped from it like a mask; he is an outlaw. "The whole order of nature is banded with God against his senseless foes"—creation, which was our friend yesterday, is to-day in alliance with the divine justice for our undoing.

It is time that we averted our eyes from this melancholy picture; let us pray that we may find, all of us, the grace of perseverance and escape that terrible sentence of an eternity spent in entire disharmony with our surroundings. Let us think about our Purgatory instead. I wonder why we are always being encouraged to think about Purgatory in connexion with our friends and so seldom encouraged to think about it in connexion with ourselves? Once more, do not let us try to picture for ourselves—how could we picture for ourselves?—a world of disembodied spirits. Let us rather consult our feelings; what will be the predominant feeling about Purgatory? Surely the sense of frustration. And by that I mean the putting out of effort which either achieves no result at all, or achieves results which are ludicrously incommensurate with the effort itself.

The sense of frustration—when you have set your heart on reaching something, and circumstances play you false; your foothold on the rock gives just as your hand is within reach, or you sink back into the mud exactly in proportion as you try to disengage yourself from it. The sense of frustration—when you feel, urgently, the need for expressing yourself, and the expression will not come; you are shouting to attract a friend's attention, and your voice will not carry, or you want to explain yourself in a hurry, and your very eagerness makes you forget the word you wanted; it is the daily tragedy of the stammerer. The sense of frustration—when it is vitally important for you to get hold of somebody, and everything goes wrong; the address can't be found, or the telephone is out of order; or perhaps you do get in touch with the person you wanted, but find that he is unexpectedly reluctant to take your point of view and to act as you had hoped; perhaps, even, someone to whom you were bound by close friendship seems to fail you; an estrangement has sprung up, and you cannot tell how.

This has always seemed to me a curious thing. When you go to bed and fall asleep, you would expect that this experience of frustration would be ruled out. In your dreams, you move in a world of pure fancy, there is no grim brick-wall of reality to run your head up against; surely in your dreams all should go well; there should be no misdirected effort; performance should go hand in hand with desire. And yet, as we all know, it's just the other way about. The sense of frustration lives on into our dreams, figures there surprisingly often, and with surprising poignancy. In your dreams, you have only to set your heart on reaching some coveted object, some place where you would like to be, for barrier after barrier, often of the most absurd kinds, to be set up between you and it. Nothing is more true to life, I mean to dream life, about *Alice in Wonderland*, than the way in which she can never get into the garden, because she is either too small to reach the key or too large to go through the door. In your dreams, the power of self-expression deserts you more fatally than ever; you want to make some statement which is of vital moment, and every time you open your lips you find that you have burst into a comic song. In your dreams, the one person you want to find is the one person who is not there; to search for that person means triumphing over innumerable difficulties, and then realizing that it is not that person you have made contact with, but somebody quite different.

Centuries ago, a pagan poet had occasion to draw a picture, from his own guess-work, of the conditions under which life might be imagined as persisting beyond the grave. If you are familiar with the sixth book of Virgil's *Aeneid*, you will probably agree that the whole of it has a certain dream quality. And the future world as he pictures it is, at least for the great mass of the people concerned, a life of frustration. Those whose bodies remain unburied on earth cannot even reach the shadowy regions which are their proper home; a river cuts them off from it. Again and again the ferry-boat plies across that river, but always, in spite of their entreaties, they are left behind. They have set their heart on getting to a particular place, and access is denied them—the old frustration. Later in the book its hero, Aeneas, meets with the spirits of certain Greek warriors who had fought against him at Troy; and these, recognizing their enemy, try to raise the war-cry among themselves and make an assault on him. But the war-cry will not come; their mouths open and the voice will not come. They feel the need of expressing themselves, and the power of expression is lacking—the old frustration. Finally, he meets his father, Anchises, and, when he bids him farewell, tries to embrace him. But it is the same story: "Thrice I tried to throw my arms round his neck, and thrice the shadowy form eluded my grasp". This interview had been the main object of his visit; he has braved innumerable perils; surely fate will not deny him the satisfaction of a single embrace at parting? But no, he cannot establish full contact with that beloved spirit—the old frustration. The most cheerful future which pagan thought could devise for its dead was a dream life in a world of dreams.

And yet, I wonder whether we may not be allowed to make use of Virgil's guess-work, when we are trying to imagine for ourselves the conditions of Purgatory? The Bible tells us so little about it, the Church has so little in the way of solid assurance to impart to us. All we know about it really is that it is a state in which disembodied spirits undergo punishment, limited in its duration, to make amends for past sins whose guilt is already forgiven. I should not be surprised if those pagan guesses are after all near the mark.

The sense of frustration—is not that, after all, exactly what we should expect to feel in Purgatory?

We shall be wanting to get somewhere, to that heaven which is our appointed home, which is in a sense, now that the guilt of our sins lies behind us, our natural home. But something, some force whose nature is unknown to us now, perhaps will be unknown to us then, will keep us back. It will not be something in ourselves; the sight of our Lord's face, made known to us in our judgement, will have made us apt for heaven, ripe for heaven, and yet heaven will elude our grasp; frustration always. We shall be eager to express ourselves, to show our love for God in meritorious action, as we formerly had the opportunity to show it, and so often neglected to show it, on earth; and there will be no faculty in us for meritorious action now. That we shall offer prayer in Purgatory is a natural assumption; but will it avail to further us on our way? Does not the insistence of the Church on the duty of praying for the dead rather suggest the contrary? The overmastering impulse in us to do something for God, and we shall not be in a position to do, only to suffer; frustration again. And, above all, we shall be aspiring to conscious union with God. Here, in a sense, you may think of the privations of Purgatory as even more searing than those of hell. The lost soul does not want God; it only feels its nature eternally unsatisfied through the loss of something which nevertheless it hates. But in Purgatory we shall want God, we shall know what it is we are going without, and that lack, though it be limited by time, will be almost intolerable. God will be just round the corner, and always unattainable. Are we right in thinking of Purgatory as waiting patiently, with folded hands, amid all we have to suffer, for a long-delayed but inevitable event? Oughtn't we rather to think of the holy souls as full, even now, of a desperate activity which can result in nothing? Frustration again.

Beyond that lies, please God, an eternity of fulfilment which shines all the brighter from contrast with the melancholy pictures we have been contemplating: instead of that disharmony, which is hell, perfect harmony with all our environment; our human nature, so full of vague dissatisfactions here, finding itself at last; instead of that frustration, which is Purgatory, a life of ceaseless activity which has no cramping limitations to make effort come painful to us; swimming in an unlaborious sea; "never they crave, but the boon hath been granted"—every aspiration is no sooner felt than it is fulfilled, and the enjoyment of every prize won is conditioned only by the ardour with which it was coveted.

VII

THE SPIRIT OF FAITH

For this meditation, we will be content with a very simple composition of place; we will go no further than the window-pane. We will think of the window-pane as it shows on some evening of early autumn, when you have not the heart to draw the curtains on the lingering afterglow of sunset, yet have to confess that you cannot get on any longer without switching on the electric light. The effect of that upon insect life is curious. You may be watching it out of idle curiosity, or for the more practical purpose of swatting the mosquitoes. But how curious it is that the ones inside, the ones you want to swat, are all making for the daylight; the ones outside, which you find yourself trying to swat by mistake now and again, are making for the glow of your electric lamp! And for the hundredth time you reflect, how odd it must be to be an insect, and not understand about glass. To spend such a large part of your time beating your wings against an insuperable obstacle, convinced, because you can't see it, that it isn't there. If there is a bit of your window open, top or bottom, the insects sail freely in and out, but only the ones which have had the luck to try that special approach. Insects, apparently, don't feel the draught as we do, or their life would be made very much simpler. They see the light ahead of them and make for it; and it is all a matter of luck whether they happen to strike the real opening, or go on for hours pushing, pushing against this mysterious obstacle which they can't believe in.

It makes rather a good parable, don't you think, if one takes the room as representing the Church, and the glass as representing that curious thing for which we have no name—that sheath of simultaneous attraction and repulsion which surrounds the Church. I want to talk about faith, and faith, not as you find it in the theological manuals, but rather as you come across it in real life. How is it that you get two people, both attracted towards the Church, both as far as you can judge in thoroughly good dispositions, and yet one of them finds the way in and the other doesn't? Oh yes, I know there is a lot to be said about that on the theological side. But take it as a matter of psychology; how do you account for those souls which seem to see their way perfectly, the whole Catholic idea is opening itself up to them, and yet at the last moment they seem to come up against a wall of glass? I say "a wall of glass" because it is something we can't account for, just as the moth which is trying to get into your room can't account for the mysterious inhibition which retards its progress.

And it isn't only on that side, is it? The unaccountable wall of glass, which makes it so hard for some people to get into the Church, makes it so hard for some people to get out of it. You know the sort of people I mean: the people who turn quite worldly and perhaps live wholly disedifying lives, get into trouble with their marriage arrangement as likely as not, and can't go to the sacraments; the Church is no longer any use to them, and it is hard to see how it can have any attraction for them, but they don't lose the faith. Of course, that is quite as it should be, from the theologians' point of view; theologically it is the most natural thing in the world for people to lose charity and yet keep the faith. But as a matter of psychology, don't you think it's very difficult to look into the mind of a person like that—to imagine why the disused faculty for religion doesn't get atrophied? But it doesn't; there they are, like butterflies beating their wings against the window-pane, unable to get out, while the moths beat theirs on the other side of it, unable to get in. Something, they don't quite know what, keeps them back.

Faith without works, the spark smouldering on among the embers, how difficult it is, at first sight, to believe in! Our non-Catholic friends don't really believe in it; the faith which lives by love is the only faith they know; lose one, and you lose the other. Or rather, if anything survives, it will be love without faith, not faith without love. It's quite difficult even for us converts to get accustomed to the idea. And yet it's not a mere figment of the theologians; it really happens. People *are* reconciled on their death-beds just as mosquitoes are swatted on the window-pane—the people who can't get out. What a bloodless, what an attenuated thing faith seems, when you think of it like that, how mysteriously folded away in some crease of the mind, unconnected with these people's daily lives, and, more strangely still, unconnected with their daily thoughts! There are so many stumbling-blocks about the Christian religion; so many loop-holes, you would have thought, by which you can get out of it, quarrelling with a doctrine there, a practice there, so as to justify yourself in saying that you refuse to be a Catholic any longer—and yet these people stick to it! What a puzzling adornment of human lives, this gift of God which goes on free-wheeling, as it were, inside our natures, doing no good, here and now, to us, giving no glory, here and now, to him! The loose-living Catholic, the loose-living free-thinker—what is there to choose between them? Just this unfunctioning organ, this dormant faculty, this pin-point of theological assertion, persisting, less because the Catholic attaches any value to it, than because he does not know how to get rid of it—like a car laid up in the garage when there is a petrol shortage, because the owner can neither use it nor sell it!

Is that all faith is?

I suppose, in the strict theological sense, yes. It is possible to have the faith, and to do nothing about it. It is far commoner to have the faith and do next to nothing about it. Let us construct another picture—not, please God, a picture of you and me, but a picture like enough to make you and me feel uncomfortable. Here is a man who is both a believing and a practising Catholic; and his belief really influences his practice—he goes to his duties, he is kind to people who are in difficulties, he puts up a fight against his temptations, in the spirit of a Christian. And yet, he is a Catholic with a difference; how shall I put it? It never comes between him and his sleep; he never takes the strain of being a Catholic. He is perfectly convinced that the Church is the only means by which, normally and as a matter of covenant, God invites people to be saved. And yet, neither the triumphs nor the set-backs of the Church really affect him. If he reads about Catholics being persecuted abroad, he clucks his tongue a bit, but supposes there is something to be said on both sides. If there's an appeal for foreign missions, he contributes to it, but wonders whether these missionary fellows really do much good; seems to him native Christians are generally rather a second-class article, from all he hears. If he learns that some friend of his is on the way to conversion, he is quite glad about it, perhaps says a prayer about it, but he doesn't particularly want it to happen; if the truth were told, he would be quite ready for So-and-so to remain as he is—he's a very good fellow. Conversely, if he hears that some friend has lost his religion, he is sorry about it—yes, but not really as sorry as if the man had had a stroke. He quite holds with monks and nuns, as long as they don't come bothering him, but he can't help thinking all that kind of thing is a bit overdone, you know. Have I contrived to give his atmosphere? Simplest, perhaps, to say that while in many ways he is a credit to his education, his point of view is as nearly as possible unsupernatural.

Our Lord says, "If you have faith, though it be but as a grain of mustard seed, you have only to say to this mountain, Remove from this place to that, and it will remove; nothing will be impossible to you." What do we mean, when we say that the saints had more faith than ourselves? The habit of faith, surely, is there or it isn't; you have lost it or you haven't. Nor did the saints believe in anything you and I don't believe in; the content of their faith wasn't greater than ours. No, but they had something which we lack—"the spirit of faith", we call it, so as to be sure that we are using language accurately. It is something other than, something over and above, that bare theological qualification which places you on this side or on that of the glass barrier.

As a matter of fact, you don't even have to go to the saints to find it. And I think sometimes it is more practical not to take the saints for our model, the saints who lived so long ago, most of them, and so hopelessly out of our reach. We get a better angle on the situation by comparing ourselves with fairly modern people who haven't been canonized—not yet, anyhow. If you take a person like Father Dominic Barberi, what can have possessed him (if that is not the wrong way of putting it) to imagine that he could come over to England, unable to talk the language, with no money and hardly any backing, and do any good when he got there? Of course, he was right; he did do a lot of good, quite apart from receiving Newman into the Church. But that doesn't help us to understand the mountain-moving psychology. And even if he was right (we're inclined to say) in guessing that England would be a possible hunting-ground for the Passionists, surely the target he set before himself was a fantastic one; he thought England was going to be converted, just like *that*, the England of Lord Brougham and Lord Macaulay! Nowadays, we are so disillusioned. The conversion of England? Oh, yes, by God's mercy that will come, one day; but of course we shan't live to see even the beginnings of that! How is it that we have lost heart, that the spirit of faith seems exiled from us?

Well, not absolutely, of course. We do still find ourselves saying, "What wonderful faith So-and-so has got!" and even, "I wish I had faith like So-and-so's." But I'm afraid there's generally a kind of arrière-pensée when we talk like that; we mean that the person in question has got a very small grasp of realities, or else a very odd idea of business. It will be an enthusiastic tertiary, who thinks if we kept a novena all over England it would be sure to convert Russia, or a Reverend Mother who has just bought a large country house and comes to us to pay off the debt on it. And that fact sometimes leads us on to the uncomfortable reflection, when we look back with envy on the past, and talk about the Ages of Faith, do we really mean that people in those days were rather stupider than we are now? That we differ from them in having more sense of realities? And if the spirit of faith means having very little sense of realities, are we quite sure that we want it?

Well, let's be honest with ourselves; I think in retreat one ought always to face the facts, not smother up one's difficulties with pious ejaculations. I do think it was humanly easier, I do not say to be a good Christian, but to be a determined, go-at-it-baldheaded sort of Christian, in days when the general outlook of the human race was more naïve than it is now. The imagination was less dominated by disconcerting reflexions; you were less side-tracked by hesitations and afterthoughts. I daresay it was easier to focus the world Christianly before Copernicus discovered that the earth went round the sun; and even (if you won't misunderstand my putting it in that way) before Columbus discovered America. Much more importantly, you could go about the business of your soul with less embarrassment before we learned, as we learned at the Renaissance, to be looking inwards all the time, to think that we weren't [in a state of] being unless we were cogitating; before, in fact, we all became so dreadfully self-conscious. But I think there is one difference between ourselves and our forefathers which has even more to do with the subject I am trying to discuss. I mean that we have become, not merely as compared with our medieval forefathers, but even as compared with our Victorian grandfathers, so desperately broad-minded.

To put it roughly, a Christian of the first seventeen centuries saw the dead heretic as probably in hell; a modern Christian sees the dead heretic as probably in heaven. The change of emphasis is there, and you cannot alter it. The Church approves or disapproves of our theological statements; wisely, and necessarily, she does not interfere with our emphasis. Our world-picture is no longer the clear-cut, Pre-Raphaelite thing it was, with a very sharp line marking off the saved from the damned; it is an impressionist affair, with the colours running into one another a good deal, an absence of violent contrasts. To convert the heretic, or even the honest unbeliever, is no longer for us the now-or-never affair it used to be. I do not say that apostolic zeal has grown cold among us; I only say that one pair of bellows which used to fan it, the idea of human souls being lost by the million, no longer blows so vigorously as it did.

Don't tell me that it is no danger to your faith and mine, living in a world like that. I don't mean our theological faith—no reason why we should start doubting articles of the creed. No, but the spirit of faith in us—the spirit we reverence in the saints, the spirit we half admire and half pity in the nuns who come begging. Without it, there can be no real zeal, and we shall remain incomplete; every Christian ought to be a zealous Christian. We're like the poor wretched government trying to make people work without appealing to the profit-motive—we've got to foster zeal in our own lives without appealing to the hell-motive; we've got to want the postman and the girl at the tobacconist's to become Catholics *without* the conviction that if they die Protestants they'll be damned. The sense of urgency which is lost to us, now that we've all become so broad-minded, has got to be replaced by a sense of urgency based on some other motive; where are we going to get it from?

I think we've got to ask Almighty God to give us more love, much more love, of his truth for its own sake. Loving the truth isn't the same thing as arguing about it; when we argue, we are so bent on getting the other person to see our point of view that we hardly mind whether it is true or not; we become advocates. Loving the truth isn't the same thing as preaching it or writing about it; when we preach it or write about it we are too much concerned with making it clear, with getting it across, to appreciate it in its own nature. Loving the truth isn't even the same thing as studying it, or meditating about it; when we study it, we are out to master it; when we meditate about it, we are using it as a lever which will help us to get a move on with the business of our own souls. No, we have got to love the truth with a jealous, consuming love that can't rest satisfied until it has won the allegiance of every sane man and woman on God's earth. And we don't, very often, love it like that. We are God's spoiled children; his truth drops into your lap like a ripe fruit—Open thy mouth wide, he says, and I will fill it. There is a sense, you know, in which the false thinkers of to-day love the truth better than Christians do. Their fancied truth is something they have earned by their own labours, and they appreciate it more than we appreciate the real truth which has dropped into our laps.

The truth of which we are speaking is not a set of abstract propositions, however august. We are to love the truth as it is in Christ; he himself is truth incarnate, and we call upon every human mind to surrender to his service—every human mind, and our own minds first; but it must be a real intellectual surrender. We are to preach the gospel, not as a mere recipe which we have tried and found useful, not as a mere pattern of living which we have learned to admire, but as truth, which has a right to be told, which would still have to be told, even if no heaven beckoned from above, no hell yawned beneath us. If we really loved the truth, then perhaps it would bite deeper into our minds, become realized and operative, not a mere set of formulas, which we accept with a shrug of the shoulders. And then perhaps we should recapture that spirit of faith, in which the men who went before us moved the world.

VIII

THE LOVE OF GOD

The Love of God—I don't mean God's Love of us, I mean our love for him—is a frightening subject. The whole business you and I have got in the world, the whole point of our being in the world at all, is to love God; all the saints, all the pious books, are agreed about that. If we aren't loving God enough, if we aren't loving him in the right way, we have got the whole thing wrong; we are missing our vocation as human beings. It is bad enough to contemplate the possibility that I may be making that sort of mistake, but much worse, if I have got to give other Christian people advice on the subject, and perhaps the wrong advice. How shall I ever forgive myself, if I encourage my fellow-Christians to be content with loving God in insufficient measure, or loving him in a way he doesn't want to be loved?

Nothing makes me so despondent on the subject as the care-free, cheerful way in which so many holy people have written about it, telling us that it's the simplest thing in the world, loving God. I have in my mind now one of the Breviary lessons from the Fathers, which tells you that Love doesn't make any demands on the feet, like going on pilgrimage, or on the hands, like doing good works, or on the eyes, like staying awake all night saying your prayers; no, it says, all you and I are told to do is to love God, and surely anybody can do *that*. Yes, but can they? And do I? And if I don't, how am I to set about doing it?

You see, it's a commandment. In fact, it is *the* commandment. Loving one's neighbour follows from it automatically; loving God gives you an appetite for loving your neighbour, just as taking a walk gives you an appetite for your food. You've got to love God with your whole heart, not just the bits of it that are left over after loving your children; with your whole mind, not just now and again when you happen to think of it; with your whole soul, not just the part of it that wants to get to heaven; your whole strength, not giving yourself a holiday now and again, and saying, "I really think it's time I had a bit of a let-up." And then, for good measure, you've got to love your neighbour as yourself.

It's the characteristic commandment of the Christian religion. I know it comes in the Old Testament; but if you will look through the Old Testament to see how often it refers to loving God, what sort of numbers of quotations will you expect to get? Thirty-three in all, and a dozen of them from Deuteronomy. Nearly all the Old Testament is about fearing God, as if that were all that could be expected of us. When it doesn't talk about fearing God it talks about seeking God, as if he were a long way away and we had to find him first before we could do anything about it. Loving God doesn't come much into the Old Testament, still less, I suppose, into the other religions of the world. But for us Christians, as I say, it is *the* thing; it's what we're here for.

Now, is there any sense in *commanding* a person to love? (Don't let's be frightened of asking these questions; let's face the whole thing out, with all its difficulties, not just smother it all up with pious phrases.) Let's put it in this way—are there any conceivable circumstances in which you would command one human being to love another human being? If I may take a concrete case, by way of making the thing clearer, do we ever command children to love their aunts?

We know that they ought to love their aunts; and yet there are a good many of them to whom it doesn't seem to come natural. But we don't find ourselves saying, "Now, Johnny, love your aunt." We tell him to kiss his aunt, to open the door for his aunt, to write to his aunt and thank her for her lovely present, because those are all things which it is in Johnny's power to do. But we all have the instinct that if Johnny does love his aunt there's no point in telling him to, and if he doesn't, no amount of telling him will make him do it. What his aunt wants is affection, and affection, surely, is a thing which you can't pump up at will. Indeed, the very word "affection" indicates that; an affection isn't something you do; it's something that happens to you. Now, why is it that we don't tell a child to love its aunt, but do tell it to love God? Is the word "love" used in two quite different senses, one of which applies to God and the other applies to human beings?

Or look at the thing in another way. Most of us, before now, have found ourselves asking the question "Do I really love God?" Once more, you don't get much help by considering what such a question would mean in relation to a human being. Suppose some young man comes to you and says, "I've met an awfully nice girl and I rather think my people would like me to marry her, but the bother is, I don't really know whether I'm in love with her; how am I to find out?" Well, we don't have to be qualified psychoanalysts to answer a question like that. We say at once: "Does the room seem to light up when she comes into it? Do you find yourself walking on air when she passes you in the street and says 'Good morning'? Would your Christian name sound perfectly splendid if it were pronounced by her voice? When you write a letter to her, do you sit sucking your pen, or do you find yourself pouring out reams of rather uninteresting information about yourself? Do you find yourself telling people how awfully nice her sister is? Do you buy yourself gramophone records of her favourite tunes?" We should all be able to think up a dozen ways of solving our friend's difficulty for him. But if we start asking ourselves the same kind of question about our attitude towards God—"Does the very thought of going to Church give me a shiver of delight? Am I longing for my friends to leave me alone so that I can kneel down and say my prayers? Do I find myself going on and on reading the Bible when I know it's time for tea?"—if we start asking ourselves *that* kind of question, it isn't long before we begin to admit that we don't love God, not in that sense.

Well, of course everybody has noticed that difficulty, and the spiritual writers have tried to clear it up for us by distinguishing between two different kinds of love, which they label "affective" and "effective". The only trouble about that distinction is that short-sighted people reading about them can't see which is which, and rather deaf people listening to sermons about them can't hear which is which. So I propose that we should make things a little easier for ourselves by re-labelling them, and calling them, instead, "spontaneous love" and "deliberate love". Those terms are not by any means accurate, but they are good enough, I think, for our present purposes. Spontaneous love is the kind of thing I have just been describing, the kind of love that gets you down in spite of yourself. The English language, in one of its rare bursts of accuracy, talks about "falling" in love; you can't help yourself, you topple over. And I think obviously the saints are people who have fallen in love with God; his grace has knocked them head over heels. Jesus Christ is thenceforward their romance. With most of us, the Love of God is not, does not seem to be, a romance. We feel, God forgive us, as if we had made a mariage de convenance, and it was up to us to make the best of it, to neglect our feelings, and live by a law of duty. That is what is meant by effective love, which I am calling deliberate love. However brutal the truth may seem, it will do no harm to remind ourselves from the outset that there is such a thing, in our ordinary human experience, as deliberate love. There are hundreds of couples living all around us who would have to admit, if they questioned themselves closely, that the bloom has rubbed off their romance. And yet, if things are not to go from bad to worse, they know that the only thing is to love deliberately—to frame their lives under the influence of a cultivated sentiment which, in their heart of hearts, they do not feel.

Now, let's be clear about this first. There are quite ordinary Christians who do at times get some touch, in their prayer, of what I have called spontaneous love. You have come across some book of devotion which so grips you that you find yourself impatient to get back to it; your thanksgiving after Communion has such a tranquillizing influence that you grudge the necessity of getting breakfast ready; happier still, you find that it is possible to go about your daily work in a mood of prayer; you are never far off from God. If you have any such experience, don't be put off by references to affective love, to spontaneous love, which seem to imply that it is something second-rate, almost certainly an illusion, and quite possibly a temptation. That is true, I should think, only of one person in ten thousand, and a bit unbalanced at that. No, these flashes of experienced love are genuine, and they are a grace. They are not a tremendously rare sort of grace; there is no need to hold on to the pew for fear you should get levitated. But thank God for them, hang on to them, make the most of them—only, remind yourself that they are perhaps destined to disappear. God will give you them as long as you need them, not longer.

More probably your experience is the opposite. You have been trying, for years and years perhaps, to live an interior life, and nothing (you are tempted to say) has come of it. You don't find that you love God better now than you did at starting, not so well, perhaps. Nothing comes out of your prayer but what you put into it, and even that isn't much. You still catch yourself, at unawares, thinking of God as a hard task-master, who must be obeyed; you do not run to serve him; you never surprise yourself doing him some little, unpremeditated service, out of love. If you treated a human creature with the same cold reserve, the same half-hearted attention, you would know by instinct that you were not in love. Well, then, are you loving God?

The answer is yes. If you are trying to love God, wanting to love God, because you are trying to love God, wanting to love God, in the measure in which you are trying to love God, wanting to love God, you *are* loving God. Loving him, that is, not with an affective, spontaneous love, but with an effective, deliberate love. Have you ever noticed how people who stammer always get their symptoms wrong? They will tell you, for instance, "I find it quite easy to talk about my b-breakfast, and my lunch, and my t-t-tea, but I find it almost impossible to talk about my d-d-d-d-d-d-dinner, because for some reason I seem quite incapable of pronouncing the letter d-d-d-d-d-d-d-dee." The obvious comment on that is, "So far from being incapable of pronouncing the letter D, you've just pronounced it about seventeen times in my hearing." They *can* pronounce the letter D, but because they think they can't, they never manage to get on with the next vowel. And there are a lot of Christians who do love God, but because they think they can't love God, never get on to the next thing—which is giving up their lives and their wills to him.

You *are* loving God, deliberately. In that sense, there is no difference between loving a person and trying to love a person. And the mistake we make—it shows the absurdity of it when you put it like that—is trying to turn our deliberate love, by some effort of our own, into spontaneous love. Of course we can't; it is in the nature of spontaneous love that it comes unbidden. But we think, "If only I meditated more, or better, the thought of God's goodness in creating me, of Jesus Christ's love in coming to redeem me, would force some response of conscious, *felt* love, even out of my stony heart." Well, of course, meditation is an excellent thing. But, you know, going on telling ourselves how grateful we ought to be to God won't really warm our hearts towards him; Aristotle warns us that thought, of itself, never moves the will. I have come across a book of meditations which tells me that I ought to love God out of gratitude because he made me a substance, not an accident. I know, it would be very tiresome to be an accident instead of a substance, but that thought doesn't melt me into tears; it ought to, but it doesn't. Or again, we think that if we knelt down and made really fervent acts of love we could hypnotize ourselves, as it were, into thinking that we were loving God, and that would make us conscious of what loving God really means. Making acts of love, to be sure, is a very useful thing to do. But it won't make us *feel* the Love of God; we have been doing it too long and too often to let it produce that kind of effect. There is a kind of prayer that hardens the will; there is no kind of prayer that turns on the tap of our affections.

Well, that's how we're fixed, and we've got to make the best of it. Most people, when they say they've got to make the best of a thing, mean that they intend to go away and have a good grouse about it. I wonder where we got that idea from? No; making the best of a thing is turning what seems at first sight a drawback into a source of positive advantage. And that's what we ought to do when God denies us the privilege of loving him affectively, spontaneously. He doesn't do that just to annoy us; God never does things just to annoy us. He means us to use it to our spiritual advantage. How are we going to do that?

I think God means it to increase our sense of mendicity. Saint Augustine tells us that we are all of us beggars, standing cap in hand at the front door of the great Householder, Almighty God. And how naturally we shall take our place in the queue, if that is our trouble, that we haven't got any love to offer him! He wants us to take our stand there, like sturdy beggars, and say, "Excuse me, I know it sounds a silly thing to say, but I haven't got any love! I'm right out of it!" It isn't exactly penitence that God asks for; after all, it's not our fault if we don't *feel* towards him as we ought to. It isn't exactly that he wants to humble us; even if we loved him as much as our Blessed Lady loved him, that would be nothing to be proud of; it is his grace that does it all. No, he wants us to feel absolutely broke; he wants to see the inside of our pockets; then, at last, he will be able to make something of us. When we don't feel love, you and I, it means that Almighty God wants us to feel our want of love. Shall we sometimes vary our prayer of acts by saying what Saint Philip Neri—Saint Philip Neri, of all people!—was never tired of saying: "My God, I don't love you one bit!"?

And it's the same, of course, with a scruple some of us are apt to feel about the duty of loving God above all things. You love him all right, but do you love him more than your husband, more than your children? It seems dishonest to say that you do. Yes, but once again you are thinking in terms of feeling; you are thinking about spontaneous love. And when God tells us to love him above all things, it's not spontaneous love he is asking for; it is deliberate love. Don't ask yourself, "What do I really feel about it?"; ask yourself,

"What should I like to be able to feel about it?" The answer to *that* question will tell you the true inclination of your will.

It's the same with another scruple, which probably wouldn't ever occur to us if we were left to ourselves, but crops up now and again as the result of our spiritual reading. What is the motive which makes me love God? Do I love him for what he is in himself, or for what I hope to get out of him, for the sake of the blessed eternity which he offers me in heaven? On the one hand, is it possible for a human creature, enjoying full mental health, to love, without the expectation of getting something out of it? On the other hand, if I love God for the sake of getting to heaven, isn't that in the last resort mere selfishness, mere cupboard-love? Fierce controversies have raged over this point; two of the greatest preachers France ever produced, Bossuet and Fénelon, fell out over it and never forgave one another. But for practical purposes there is no difficulty in the matter at all. Don't ask yourself, "What is the motive for which I love God?" Ask yourself, "What is the motive for which I should like to love God?" And if you would like to love God for himself, then you do love God for himself. It is a matter of the will.

Our Lord said to Saint Thomas, "Blessed are those who have not seen, and yet have believed." I dare to hope that he will say to some of us, meeting us in heaven, "Blessed are those who have not felt, and yet have loved."

HOLY HOUR—A HIDDEN GOD

i

Isaiah says (45:15), "Truly thou art a God of hidden ways". I want you to consider how God hides himself in four connexions: in his creation, in his dealings with men, in his Incarnation, and finally in the Holy Eucharist. And I want you to see the four attitudes which that challenge is meant to evoke from us: our faith, our confidence, our humility, and finally our resignation.

God hides himself in his creation; or rather, he reveals himself in his creation, but in such a way that it is possible not to see him. He does not deceive us, but he allows us to deceive ourselves. We all know the five proofs which philosophy gives us of the existence of God, and we all know that those proofs are cogent, even if we had no other light, the light of conscience for example, to illustrate them further. And yet it only needs a certain obstinacy of the mind to look God's creation in the face and steadily refuse to go back beyond it or argue upwards from it. Man has the dreadful power of refusing to think. And for the most part when people do that they are only rationalizing what is really an attitude of the will; their will is enslaved to God's creatures and therefore their mind will not raise itself above God's creatures. For these people, then, God hides himself. And for us too, who believe, he is in a sense hidden; for we know him not in himself but only by his effects; we only see as it were the robe which he wears, not himself; and even of that robe we only see the lining—of how much poorer stuff this visible creation is made, as compared with his invisible creation! He plays a kind of hide-and-seek with us; we have to keep on looking, or we shall miss him. Even when we are nearest to him in our prayer we are only conscious of his presence as something evanescent, like the feeling you have when you enter an empty room that somebody has just left.

Why does he do that? To challenge our faith. I am using the word in the broad, not in a strictly theological sense. He allows men, if they will, to doubt his existence—he, whose very essence is to exist—in order that we who do believe in him may feel the strain all the time, keep our heads upstream, not go stale, as we are apt to do in this probationary world, for the lack of effort. To seek his presence, still more to live as in his presence, is going to cost us something; we do not value things properly unless they cost us something. How are we going to set about finding him, we who are so weak, so rudimentary in our prayer?

I always like that phrase which you come across immediately after the story of the Fall, when our first parents hid themselves in the garden from the presence of God. "They heard the voice of the Lord God walking in the garden at the afternoon air"; just that moment, I suppose, towards sunset when a hush seems to fall over nature; in London and New York they call it "the rush hour". It's as if that moment in the first cool of the evening was, in Paradise, a kind of tryst God kept with man; conscious as they were of his presence at all times in their innocency, it was then that he made himself known specially, as a mother sends for her children during the hour before they go to bed. And on that miserable day when they sinned and knew that they had sinned, they hid themselves from the presence of the Lord God among the trees of the garden. They did, you see, what we are always doing: plunged themselves into the midst of creatures in order to forget their Creator. But he called them, even so.

We are all accustomed, if and as we can, to begin the day with God; it is well that we should. But some of the spiritual authors, including I think Saint Francis de Sales, tell us that this hour in the early evening is, for some souls at least, the best time for the practice of interior prayer. Do not let us despise this practice of seeking for God's presence at some time in the late afternoon. It is then, I think, that it is easiest for some of us to shut our ears to the voice of creatures, and cultivate, though it only be for less than half an hour, the sense of God's presence; he will call, "Where art thou?" and no sense of unworthiness shall make us hide ourselves from him.

ii

"Truly thou art a God of hidden ways"; God hides himself, all the time, in his dealings with us men. After all, we should have expected, and mankind has always expected, that he would single out his own servants for particular favour; that a nation, a family, an individual who served him faithfully would prosper, even in this life, more than their neighbours—be a standing advertisement to posterity that it is worth while to serve God. And of course now and again in history, when you read of the victories won by Constantine, or Clovis, or Charlemagne, you are tempted to think, "Well, that's all right; evidently, God does protect his own." But that mood of satisfaction doesn't last long. You haven't to go far to find instances in which a Catholic state has gone under, or years of patient work spent in building up a magnificent edifice of Catholic organization has been demolished at a blow. And so it is when you observe individual lives; how was it that So-and-so, who tried so hard to do God's will and live in his sight, was allowed to be the victim of continual misfortune? And even in your own life, was it when you tried hardest that you were most rewarded? No; God hid himself, would not allow you to trace, as if by a mechanical process of cause and effect, the connexion of his favours with your endeavours for him.

Just as we saw that God, in creating the world, left it open to us, if we would, to lose faith, so in his governance of the world God leaves it open to us, if we will, to lose hope. He lays himself open to the blasphemy of those who say, "Well, if God does exist, he is either singularly limited in his powers or singularly wanting in watchfulness over the innocent and the devout." I always like the story of Saint Theresa, when she was carried away by the force of the stream while fording a river; if you remember, she felt our Lord holding her down under the water and heard him saying, "This is how I treat my faithful servants"; and Saint Theresa, with a kind of holy cynicism of which only she would have been capable, answered, "That, O Lord, is why thou hast so few." God hides himself when we are in difficulties; how often we feel that! How often the Jews felt it; "Lord, why dost thou stand far off? In days of peril and affliction, why dost thou make no sign?" And, what makes it worse, as if to emphasize this neglect, this seeming neglect, he encourages us to pray to him, tells us to ask him for everything we want, like children asking bread from their father; and then we pray, and nothing happens! How many despairs, how many blasphemies, he incurs by treating us as he does!

What is the secret of it? Well, of course, there is one account of it which is easily given the moment you reflect on the possibilities; it is the answer given in the book of Job. Doth Job serve God for naught? asks the accusing angel; and it is when Job has lost everything he held dear, and serves God still, that the devil's lie is retorted on him. If piety always obviously paid, it would not be long before people took to being pious simply for what they could get out of it. But, as that story of Saint Theresa suggests, there is a deeper meaning still. Do you remember how Elijah, after he had triumphed over the false prophets of Baal, was hunted out by Queen Jezebel and fled for his life into the wilderness, how he came to Mount Horeb and made his complaint to God there? "I am all jealousy" (he says), "for the honour of the Lord God of hosts; see how the sons of Israel have thrown down thy altars, and put thy prophets to the sword; of these, I only am left, and now my life, too, is forfeit." And then the Lord God passes by. "A wind there was, rude and boisterous, that shook the mountains and broke the rocks in pieces before the Lord, but the Lord was not in the wind; and after the wind an earthquake, but the Lord was not in the earthquake; and after the earthquake a fire, but the Lord was not in the fire, and after the fire the whisper of a gentle breeze." It was as a silent whisper that Elijah heard God's voice and learned that all the passionate entreaties by which he had tried to storm heaven were misplaced; that it was in stillness he must wait for God; that prayer means, not bending God's will to ours, but bending our will to God's. God hides himself from us in his governance of the world, and of our own lives, that we may learn to give up our own wills, and want, in life and in death, only what he wants, knowing that it is best for us. As we have made our act of faith in his presence, let us make now our act of confidence in his will.

iii

"Truly thou art a God of hidden ways." God hides himself in his Incarnation, not becoming merely man for us, but becoming a little child, a poor man, derided by his enemies, condemned to death as an impostor, dying a slave's death and at last lying in the tomb—God hidden not as man merely, but as a dead man.

Of course, just as it is true that God reveals himself in his creation, so it is true that he reveals himself in his Incarnation. As a candid mind which will fix itself upon the considerations which lie open to it ought to learn, from contemplation of the world around it, the existence of its Creator, so a candid mind reading the story of the Gospels and weighing the effect on history of what happened in Galilee hundreds of years ago, ought to see in the Incarnation God revealed afresh, revealed more intimately than ever. But you can, if you will, withhold your assent from the cogency of that reasoning process; people did, and do. In the Incarnation, as in creation, God is half revealed and half concealed; that is the point. He revealed himself, but not in a way to startle or to cow the imagination. "He will not strive nor cry out", the prophet wrote of him; "none shall hear his voice in the streets". Our Lord would be born, not as a Roman emperor but as a Galilean peasant; would live, not as a philosopher courted by all the sages of his time, but as a street-corner orator, producing a nine-days' wonder among the fisher-folk of Capernaum; would die, not as a martyr but as an impostor; would rise again, to show himself only to a handful of friends and return whence he came, leaving the world to forget him if it would, to doubt him if it would.

Oh yes, he did miracles, staggering miracles, in the presence of a great concourse of people sometimes. But he did them among his friends and his followers; when the Pharisees asked him for a sign, there was no sign forthcoming. True God, in his Incarnation he hides himself as much as possible behind the veil of his humanity; he will not even allow himself to be called good—there is none good, he says, save God. You might almost say that he courts misrepresentation—eats with publicans and sinners to hide his sinlessness, agonizes in the garden to dissemble his omnipotence. There is nothing so divine about our Lord, if I may use a paradox, as his humanness; as Creator, he hides himself behind his creation, as Incarnate, he hides himself in a creature-nature—it is a touch of the same artist's brush.

Why did he do that? Partly, of course, in order to exercise our faith; conviction should not force itself upon the mind; there should be a loop-hole, once again, by which doubt could creep in, if men were resolved to doubt. But it was partly to teach us a lesson of humility, of self-annihilation. He annihilates himself, as far as that is possible, when you see him as a baby at his Mother's breast; that is the point of the devotion to the sacred infancy. The devotion to the sacred infancy is not a sort of pretty-pretty affair, accommodating itself to our modern, sentimental pose of making a great fuss about children; it is based on the amazing reflexion that Omnipotent Godhead did hide itself in the form of a speechless, helpless Thing wrapped about in swaddling-clothes, needing to have everything done for it, needing to be fed, to be protected, to be taught, all the time. If God annihilated himself like that, how ought we to annihilate ourselves before God? And when he lies in the sepulchre, it is not simply that we might weep over the cruel hurts which brought him there; it is that we might see the timeless, passionless, immutable Word of God hidden in the form of a dead thing—Divine Personality united to a corpse.

As a child in the womb, as a corpse in the tomb, he appeals to us to obliterate ourselves, to annihilate ourselves. We, who are nothing, must learn our own nothingness, must learn to kill all that spirit of self-pleasing and self-assertion which mixes itself up even with our best desires, even with our most altruistic actions. We must learn, not merely to will what he wills, but to will what he wills only because he wills it; to make ourselves his tools, his playthings; die to ourselves that he may live in us.

iv

"Truly thou art a God of hidden ways"—God hides himself still more effectively, still more intimately, in the Holy Eucharist. Indeed, you may say that this mystery sums up and exceeds those other mysteries which we have been considering.

God hides himself in creation, in the sense that you cannot read in it the evidence to prove his existence unless you will use your reason over it. If you will use it, reason points to God as surely as the compass points to the magnetic pole. But where he hides himself in the Holy Eucharist, reason gives no indication, is powerless to infer. It can tell us, what the senses cannot tell us, that there is an underlying reality which sustains, in natural objects, those outward appearances which impress themselves on our senses. But, that when the priest has spoken the words of Consecration, the reality of Christ's Body and Blood becomes present—over all that reason has no message to give us; nothing, here, will point to God's presence except the divining-wand of faith. If, then, God as hidden in creation allows men, easily and frequently, to blaspheme him by saying there is no God, so, as hidden in the Holy Eucharist, he allows men, still more easily, still more frequently, to blaspheme him by saying there is no God here. More effectively than ever he shrouds himself from profane eyes, that he may reveal himself more effectively than ever to the eyes of faith. When we honour him in his Sacrament, we have to make reparation not only for the many who deny his existence, but for those, still more numerous, who deny his sacramental presence.

God hides himself in his governance of the world, in the sense that he does not ordinarily allow us to see which are his chosen friends by singling them out for special favours. He makes his sun rise on the evil and equally on the good, his rain fall on the just and equally on the unjust. But his operation upon men's souls when he comes to them in the sacrament of Holy Eucharist is still more jealously hidden. The Holy Eucharist is a sun which fosters supernatural life in those who receive it worthily, rain which gives them growth. It is a sun which dries up all life in the souls which receive it unworthily, rain which brings with it only corruption. But all this is hidden from our knowledge; we cannot tell whether the gift brings life or death to the communicant who is kneeling next to us. In his operation, as in his presence, God hides himself here, more effectively than ever.

And if, in his Incarnation, God stooped towards us and condescended to our level by uniting his Divine Nature with a human nature, which, though created, was created in his image, was part of his spiritual creation, how much lower he stoops, how much more he condescends, when he hides himself in the Holy Eucharist, veiled under the forms of material, insensible things! If in his Incarnation he gave himself up into the hands of men, allowed them to overpower him and control his movements, how much more generously does he give himself in the Holy Eucharist, putting himself in the priest's hands and exposing himself to sacrilege at the whim of his enemies! Hidden not only from sense but from reason, hiding from us not only the principle on which he bestows his benefits but the actual bestowal of them, yielding himself to us not merely in the form of a servant, as in his Incarnation, but in the form of an instrument, available at our will, surely he finds in the Holy Eucharist the best hiding-place of all.

And what attitude should all that provoke on our side? Surely one of utter resignation into his hands. Our Lord, in the Tabernacle, puts himself at our disposal, ready for our worship, if we will come to worship him, ready to give life to our souls, if we will receive him, but all the time, however we neglect him, offering himself as a Victim to his heavenly Father. We on our side are to put ourselves entirely at his disposal—ready to do all he would have us do, ready to suffer all he would have us suffer, but all the time, whether he calls upon us for such service or not, offering ourselves as victims to the same heavenly Father, in harmony with his aspiration, and in union with his sacrifice.

IX

OUR LORD AND THE RICH YOUNG MAN

In that pregnant, packed bit of writing, whose numerous points we continually miss because we are so familiar with the sound of the words, the prologue to Saint John's Gospel, the sentence occurs, "He came to his home, and his own family did not welcome him." That is Goodspeed's translation, and I think it gives you the stab of the sentence better than most others. Only it is perhaps a little daring, when the Second Person of the Blessed Trinity becomes incarnate on earth, to describe him as coming home. But it gets the point, the point which stands out so clearly if you try to read through the Old Testament. Once you get beneath the surface of the Old Testament, so largely disedifying, so largely unattractive to the reader, you can see, all down the centuries, an intensive work of preparation going on, for one particular event. The thunders of Sinai are the artillery meant to soften just this one particular point in Satan's defences. The corpses piled up in such profusion are so much manure meant to fertilize this one particular plot of the earth's surface. The sudden snatches of hundred per cent spirituality which keep on cropping up here and there in the Old Testament, taking your breath away, are the soft twigs and leaves out of which a nest is being built for the Heavenly Dove to find a refuge at last, after all the desolation the deluge has left behind it. I always regret the two books of Maccabees being put in where they are, because it spoils the whole crescendo effect Malachi makes on you. Malachi is the last book of the Old Testament; "Here am I sending my messenger to prepare the way for thy coming"; everything's ready for zero hour; the land was never in such good heart; the nest is all finished, down to the last detail: *now*!

And then, humanly speaking, the terrible fiasco which followed! The people who wanted to see our Lord [are] always the *wrong* people: the Wise Men coming to adore while Herod is plotting to murder him; the Greeks coming up to Saint Philip with their "Sir, we would see Jesus", on the very eve of his Passion! We are going to talk about our Lord's earthly life, and of course the subject is infinite; even if you think about our Lord's earthly life as a model and an inspiration for us, his miserable servants, the subject is infinite. You must select, you must classify, you must clarify your material. So I thought we would confine our attention to this single, salient fact about our Lord's life, which Saint John writes down so ruthlessly on the very threshold of it; he came home, and his own family did not welcome him. How terribly often one heard, during the war, of a soldier who came back from the wars to find that he was not wanted! The wife—God forgive us all, what horrible creatures we are!—had got tied up with another man, and the fireside, dreamed of among desert sands or Burmese swamps, had become a cold hearth in the meantime; just where the man *ought* to have been welcome, he was one too many. When we have exhausted our indignation over that familiar picture, let's remind ourselves that this was, in effect, the experience of Incarnate God. His own people, his Bride, as the prophets loved to think of it, had no use for him, could make no room for him in its twisted habit of thought. "I was sought by those who found me not"—the prophets had always been foretelling it. The people our

Lord came to redeem in the first instance, not all of them, but as a people, rejected him, and reject him still.

We can't, I suppose, in the common meaning of the word, say that our Lord Jesus Christ was ever disappointed. Because in our experience disappointment means the unexpected happening, and the unexpected could not happen to him. But I think it is quite obvious that he had the feeling of disappointment—of wishes frustrated, of endeavours thrown away. "Jerusalem, Jerusalem, how often I would have gathered your children, as a hen gathers her chickens under her wings, and you refused"—that tone of melancholy is, you may say, the leit-motif of the Gospels. It isn't so, after all, with the lives of the saints; when you read the life of a saint, you expect to be told about all the people the holy man succeeded in converting, the people who at first opposed him, but were afterwards won over by his gentleness and patience. But with our Lord's life it is just the other way; we are continually being confronted with his failures. "After this, many of his disciples went back to their old ways, and walked no more in his company"—what a dreadful admission! In his own town of Nazareth he is unhonoured; he "cannot" (whatever that means) do many miracles there, because of their unbelief; and these were the people who should have been so proud of him! Not even his kinsmen believed in him—just the people who ought to have known him best! And then there are the nine lepers who never come back to give thanks, and the three would-be disciples who turn out, after all, to be wouldn't-be disciples. And even in the training of his own apostles what a lot of set-backs there are: the want of faith, the want of patience, the want of humility, and then Saint Peter's denial as a kind of signature-tune at the end of it all! How our Lord's own teaching reflects the mood of a disappointed man: the crops that come to nothing; the people who bury their talents in napkins, or say they will work in the vineyard and then don't, or accept invitations to the wedding and then send word at the last moment that they can't be there; the fish that have to be thrown back into the sea as uneatable; the people who keep on saying "Master, master" and then do nothing about it—was there ever a Teacher so haunted by the sense of failure?

And, of course, there was Judas Iscariot, always at his elbow. But I think of all the pictures in the Gospels which represent our Lord as thwarted in his human contacts, none is more poignant than the account given in Saint Mark of the rich young man. Do you remember what he says—the other evangelists haven't the courage to say it? He says, "Jesus fastened his eyes on him, and conceived a love for him." Well, we don't know that the rich young man came to grief in the end. He may have been Joseph of Arimathea; he may have been Saint Paul himself. But I think our instinct is that the refusal then made was made once for all. And yet this was the man our Lord loved, the only individual described in that way by the Gospels, except Saint John, and the family at Bethany. Our Lord looked him well in the eyes and conceived a love for him; that is the plain meaning of the Greek. He saw qualities there which brought out all his human capacity for affection; this was the kind of person you would be glad to do something for, a nature capable of great generosity, and needing to be treated on a heroic level: "Go and sell all thou hast, and give to the poor." And we, coming fresh from reading the lives of the saints, think we know the inevitable sequel: "The young man was so deeply impressed by these unexpected words that he went straight home, sold all that he had, and afterwards became one of the most edifying of our fathers"—that must be it, surely? No; he went away sorrowing, for he had great possessions. Looked at and loved by the Saviour of the world, and he turns out a failure!

I think it's probably true to say that, while life in this fallen world is a disappointing experience in many ways, the most searing disappointments we encounter are due to the interaction of other people's lives with our own. You can put the reason quite briefly thus. Being human, we are fonder of some people than of others. Being human, we inevitably try to influence the people we are fond of. And, whether by some mysterious law, or just by some piece of bad luck, the people we are fondest of are not, as a rule, the people who improve most under our influence.

I know all that sounds frightfully pompous; I must beg you to understand that I'm not thinking of those people with a real love of interference who go about the world continually trying to arrange other people's lives for them, and commonly deserving all the disappointments they get. Nor when I talk of influencing other people do I mean, necessarily or chiefly, trying to correct their faults. More probably we try to bring out, to encourage, the best in them—as our Lord did with the rich young man. He must have had some faults, but our Lord didn't bother about those; he wanted to start him straight on the counsels of perfection. So it is when *we* are fond of people; we want them to live up to our ideal of them; we want them to develop the good qualities we have discovered in them; we want them to appreciate the same things, the same people, as ourselves. And, conversely, if it is part of your work in life to influence other people, you almost inevitably become fonder of some than of others. The teacher has his favourite pupils; the parish priest finds himself worrying more about the spiritual welfare of two or three people in his congregation than about the rest; the mother, even, finds out that she has favourites among her own children, though she is very careful not to let anybody else find it out. So it's the commonest thing in the world to be fond of somebody, and for that reason to be trying to influence them in the right direction, to have day-dreams about it, make plans about it. And as you get older and have less life of your own to live, you are more than ever apt to live in other people's lives: the parent in the child, the teacher in his clever pupil, the priest in that girl who is going to make such a splendid nun, and so on.

And of course, we are asking for trouble. *The Imitation of Christ* asks us, in that cynical way it has, How do you expect to be a success in running other people's lives, when you see what a failure you are in running your own? How familiar the feeling is, even when we are trying to deal with our own bad habits, our own laziness or ill-temper, that the self we are trying to deal with is a different person from ourselves, or anyhow a different animal—a dog that simply won't lie down, a horse that simply won't go straight! And then, fresh from that experience of not being able to impose our own will on ourselves, we try to impose it on other people! Naturally we let ourselves in for disappointment. What a lot of sorrow is caused in the lives of good people, of good Christian people anyhow, by this refusal, on the part of those they love, to run according to schedule! What a lot of non-Catholic husbands you meet, full of honesty, full of good will, happily married to exemplary Catholics, who still don't get the grace of faith! What a lot of Catholic parents whose children, on growing up, have run wild, or have lost touch, somehow, with their religion! We all know the story of Saint Ambrose, when Saint Monica was almost in despair about the false direction taken by her son Augustine, assuring her, "It is not possible that the child of so many tears should perish." Does that really seem true to our experience? And if not, how dreadful that the very unselfishness which makes us want to live in and for others should itself be an instrument that tortures us!

What shall we say to them, the people whose very tenderness of heart makes life a purgatory for them? Three things, I think, in any case.

First, let them reflect that they are undergoing an experience which our Lord himself has hallowed by his example. And, remember, it was all the worse for him in proportion as his heart was larger, as his sympathies had a wider range than ours. He was disappointed in the rich young man, not merely for his own sake but because he stood as a type of the whole nation to which he belonged. "Jerusalem, Jerusalem, still murdering the prophets!"—here was this people of the Jews, so pathetically loyal, at least in external ways, to the divine law delivered on Mount Sinai; "all these commandments I have kept from my youth up". This people of the Jews, with such splendid qualities of tenacity, of discipline, of God-fearingness! And now it is called upon to rise to the heights of its own vocation; "go and sell all thou hast, and give to the poor"—it is called upon to share, with the despised Gentiles, those treasures of divine revelation, divine sonship which had been lavished upon it; and it is going to fail at the test. We, whose hearts have a narrower range, find it difficult to see anything but our own immediate disappointments. But we want to ask, I think, for an enlargement of our view. We want our own tragedies to make us more sensitive to all the tragedies of the world around us, not shut us up in ourselves. We want to see, in the infidelities of those we love, not so much the danger of their loss, which touches us so nearly, but the slight, the indignity done to God's honour, not by this situation merely but by a thousand other situations just like it. If we want to lighten our disappointment by getting our Lord to share it with us, we must aspire to lighten all *his* disappointments by sharing them with him.

Second, let them never imagine, for a moment, that because the prayers they offer, the efforts they make, are not producing the result which is intended, therefore they are producing no result at all. After all, think what was the sequel to the story we have been thinking about, the story of the rich young man. He went away sorrowing; the incident, you would think, was closed; the refused invitation might just as well never have been made. Two hundred and fifty years passed, and those words, read out in church, reached the ears of another rich young man; he went straight out of church, sold all that he had, and went to live in the desert—Saint Anthony, the great eternal model of Christian monasticism. Much oftenest, I think, you will find that our influence is most powerful where it is least direct, where we had no intention of exercising it. We are so curiously built, that the thing we are especially bent on doing is the thing we fail to do; we think too much about it, hesitate, lose our nerve, and make a mess of it. Nothing is more common, I think, in any kind of pastoral work than to find that you have failed over the people you specially wanted to make a good job of, and meanwhile you have made an impression on somebody you didn't suspect of taking any notice. I've been told by an old priest, and I think a good many would tell you the same, that when he wanted to beat up his parishioners to their duties he always had a mission to non-Catholics, and when he wanted to make converts he always asked a Redemptorist in to give the parish hell. I don't know whether it is some weakness in ourselves, or whether Almighty God, jealous for his own honour, prefers to achieve his results by indirect rather than by direct influence. But be sure all the prayers we say, all the efforts we make, are having some effect, somewhere.

And third, don't let them wish, or try, to be *less* sensitive to the needs of others, to worry less about others, than their nature bids them. Our natures differ very much about that, obviously; some people are worriers, some aren't; some find it much easier than others to shrug their shoulders and say, "Well, it can't be helped; I've done my best." A priest will often be tempted to wish that he were less of a man and more of a machine—that he could learn to deliver admonitions with the same splendid impartiality with which the postman delivers the letters every morning, to bestow absolution with the same automatic aloofness which the man in the booking-office shows, behind that grille which is so like the grille of a confessional. But he is wrong. Our natures are given us so that we may make the best of them, not, apart from very exceptional cases, so that we may alter them altogether. If you have the kind of pastoral instinct which makes you worry a lot about other people's souls, don't let it lead you to neglect your own; don't let it betray you into a morbid habit of wanting to interfere here, there, and everywhere. No, but follow your own instincts; some people will have a special interest for you, will make a special claim on your sympathies; don't resist that attraction: it is all part of the nature God has given you, and therefore of the destiny God has arranged for you. But be prepared to make a mess of things; you probably will. Probably, as I say, the good you do will be something quite different, something you never intended—as likely as not something you will never hear about. But do what your hand finds to do; and then, when you are alone with God in your prayer, tell him that you want to be of use to those souls he means you to be of use to, those and no others. Tell him that you are ready to work for him blindfolded, and wait till the Day of Judgement before you ask what the result of your work was.

X

OUR LORD'S DISREGARD OF APPEARANCES

We are accustomed to divide up the life of our Blessed Lord on earth into two sections, his hidden and his public life. What I want to suggest in this meditation is that we must not press that distinction too strictly. All through his ministry our Lord was living a public life in the sense that he was, almost continuously, in the public eye. Yet his was surely a hidden life in the more intimate and more important sense that he never sought for reputation—was not even at pains to vindicate his reputation when men spoke ill of him. He was content, all through, to remit his motives to the scrutiny of his heavenly Father; there was nobody else whose opinion mattered. That inwardness in his calculations was something that should arouse our interest and challenge our imitation.

You see, we men are very curious people. Each of us, in his heart of hearts, thinks he is right. We seldom take other people's advice, unless it chimes in pretty accurately with the decision we had already formed on our own account. Yet we care desperately what other people think; we cannot be satisfied with the self-approval of our own conscience; we must for ever be justifying ourselves in the eyes of our fellow men. If we have done something which involves us in general unpopularity, we nevertheless point to a circle of friends, people who really know us, and reflect that here at least our motives are better understood. If we have written a book, and it doesn't sell, we take refuge in the approval of a small literary clique, or, it may be, a small literary claque, which still thinks the world of us; and "these", we tell ourselves, "are the people whose opinion is really worth having". At the very worst, if we are held up to scorn by the common condemnation of our fellow men, we fall back on the judgement of posterity; "years hence", we say, "the world will see these events in a saner perspective, and then I shall come into my own"— As if posterity mattered! "I do not look for honour from men", our Lord tells us. "I am not looking to my own reputation; there is another who will look to it, and be the judge." He has God's approval, and in that lonely confidence he goes through the world, asking no sympathy from us.

That is a very extraordinary attitude on his part. After all, we ask, had he not come to save the world? And how was he to save the world, if he made no effort at all to impress it, if he left it quite easy for men to ignore his claims altogether, or to set them aside as the claims of a madman? He told his apostles that they were the light of the world, and added that you do not light a lamp and then cover it over with a great can, you want it to give light all over the house. And they, he told them explicitly, must let their light shine before men; their good works must be open to view. He too, and in a special sense, claimed to be the Light of the World; ought not he, with all the greater reason, to have taken care to impress people round him? How else were they to have a chance of believing in him? Yes, all that's true, and it's clear, absolutely clear, that the people who rejected him rejected him through their own fault. If there was anything to be made of you, money-grubbing Zacchaeus or pleasure-loving Magdalen though you might be, he would make the most of it—not for him to snap the staff that was already crushed, or put out the wick that still smouldered. And yet he wouldn't protest and cry out; his voice shouldn't be heard in the streets—he was not going to be a public man. Somehow, with infinite wisdom, he contrived to be always at the disposal of the souls that really needed him, to have crowds of people hanging there on his lips, waiting there to be healed, and yet to avoid all that we mean by publicity. He had no public relations officer to make good his position before the world; the world must take him as it found him.

How his silence puzzles us! We have read about some great miracle of healing, and at the end of it he says, "Go thy way, and tell thy friends what great things the Lord has done for thee"; that we can understand; he has come to manifest his Father's glory, and deeds like this must not be done in a corner. Then, the next moment, he will send some leper away cured with strict orders that he is to tell no one about it; what is the sense of trying to hush it all up? It is too late; the whole world is talking of him. But no, there is a kind of reticence about him which comes out at what seem the most inappropriate moments. How his enigmatic habit of speech puzzles us! When he is talking to the crowds in Galilee, he utters parable after parable, and then tells his disciples afterwards, "Of course, they won't understand a word of what I'm saying—it's you who have got to do that." But why preach to them at all, we ask, if they are going to get it all wrong? And so it is with all those long arguments in Jerusalem; quite obviously our Lord and his audience are at cross purposes; he uses a kind of cipher language which is plain enough to us, but wasn't plain to them. He talks about his Father; who was his Father? He doesn't tell them. He says, "I am going back to him who sent me"; where is that? They don't know. "Whither I go, you cannot come", he tells them, and they think he must mean he is going abroad into some Gentile land. Evidently there were some of them who put two and two together and began to see what it was all about; Nicodemus was one, and Caiphas was another. But what were the rest of them about, that they understood so little? And how much were they to blame for not understanding? All that puzzles us; and I suppose the most we can say is that for some reason of his own Almighty God wanted the truth to dawn very slowly on people's minds, so that they could take it in gradually, in the measure in which each of them was prepared to receive it.

If our Lord seems to impair the effectiveness of his mission by keeping too quiet about it, or by delivering his message in terms which people can't understand, we must suppose that he had some good reason for doing so. But what is even more difficult to account for, when you read the story as if you were approaching it for the first time, is what you may call his deliberate disregard of appearances. He is always shocking his fellow countrymen by doing the wrong things, the things they have been taught not to do. Here is this ancient people of the Jews, whose whole notion of religion is bound up with the law of Moses. It has been their ideal of life for centuries; they have gone through unheard-of persecutions rather than be false to it. Oh, no doubt the provisions of the law have grown more complicated and more exacting as time went on; that is the nature of law everywhere. No doubt, through poring over it and brooding over it for so long, its most fanatical supporters, the Pharisees, have developed an outlook of legalism. But it is the best light they have, and they are, on the whole, the most conscientious part of the nation. Now, why is it that our Lord is always going out of his way, or so it seems, to flout their favourite scruples? Always telling people to carry their beds on the sabbath day, when you weren't allowed to carry burdens on the sabbath day; sitting down to meat without the ceremonial washing of hands that had become customary; surrounding himself with publicans and sinners, with people who had almost lost their consciousness of Jewish nationality, who imitated the Gentiles' ways and did the Gentiles' work for them? Only once, I think, does he show any tenderness for the characteristic prejudices of his own people, and that is when he finds means, by a miracle, to pay his dues for the upkeep of the Temple. On that occasion he does say, "We mustn't shock them, must we?"—but it is the only time. Why did our Lord want to come to earth as a Jew, and then throw overboard all these cherished observances of Judaism?

It was, surely, because he saw one failing, among several others, as characteristic of the Jewish nation in his day. They had too much regard for appearances; they were always bothering about what other people would say. And he saw that this failing was not confined to the Jewish nation; it is common to the human race as a whole, and it is uncommonly common to you and me. Against that background of shams and pietisms, the straightforwardness of his nature revolted. It was one of the lessons he came to teach us, that this craving for the good opinion of others is a disastrous thing—*one* of the lessons he came to teach us; there were lots of others; we mustn't fall into the common mistake of emphasizing a single strand of his teaching and forgetting all the rest. Against the people who were ready to clean the outside of cup and dish, the part that showed, leaving the inside to go dirty, against the people who made long prayers and swallowed up the property of widows while they were doing it, he fulminated in accents of satire that have passed into the vocabulary of the human race. And he would be contemptuous of appearances, in protest against the spirit which thinks of appearances and nothing else.

How full of human respect he sees us! Not that he wants us to be careless about our actions, and give scandal to other people; the last thing in the world he is inclined to pardon is scandal wilfully given. And I daresay it was for that reason that the incident about Saint Peter and the coin in the fish's mouth has been preserved to us. "We mustn't shock them; take a florin and pay the temple tribute for both of us!" I don't think there's any irony about what he says, only, dare we say it? I think that phrase "We mustn't shock them" is uttered without enthusiasm; it's a permission rather than a command; our Lord hasn't really got his heart in it. He would have preferred a world in which you did what you thought right and nobody took you up wrong and got bothered in conscience about it. I have the same feeling about Saint Paul; he is desperately concerned not to give scandal to other people, but I think he chafes at the necessity. "Yet for myself, I make little account of your scrutiny, or of any human audit-day; I am not even at pains to scrutinize my own conduct. My conscience does not, in fact, reproach me, but that is not where my justification lies; it is the Lord's scrutiny I must undergo"—that is, so to speak, Saint Paul at home. You and I have got to avoid conduct which will unnecessarily offend the consciences of other people; we have even got the duty of edifying other people, though I think it's a dreadful word, as commonly used. Priests have got to edify their flocks; parents have got to edify their children; school-masters and school-mistresses, God help us, have got to edify their pupils. All that is in the day's work, and we shall not be judged very hardly, I fancy, for looking more pious than we felt when we were in church. All that, at the worst, won't do nearly as much harm as the hidden root of human respect from which so many of our daily actions proceed.

You've only to watch yourself half an hour in conversation to see the thing at work. You make some absurd mistake (for instance); how quick you are to cover it up by saying you confused this with that, you were thinking of this or that which of course isn't quite the same, anything to save your face! Dr. Johnson, when a lady asked him how he came to make some mistake in his dictionary, replied, "Ignorance, Madam, stark ignorance." You and I haven't, commonly, the honesty to say that. And what a picture it gives of the inside of our minds! I don't mean the insincerity of it; that isn't what concerns us just now; but how extraordinary that we should *mind* so much about the opinion other people are going to form of us! We are living our lives all on the surface. "My eyes are ever fixed on the Lord", wrote King David, and we would like ours to be, but instead of keeping our gaze fixed on him we are always looking round at one another, like school-girls in church. If we were really Christians, we should be very ready to take the advice of our fellow men *before* adopting this course of action or that. But, once the thing was done, the question, whether it was the right thing to do, or whether it was done with the right motives, would be a question only for ourselves and our confessor; what other people thought of us (for good or evil) wouldn't matter; why should it? We are as God sees us. That is what's really wrong about human respect; it's the habit of asking "What *will* people say?" If we cultivate it, if we live for human applause, we fall under the condemnation of those Pharisees who "valued their credit with men higher than their credit with God".

Our Lord gave us an example of disregarding appearances in his life; he gave us a further example of it in his death.

Looking at his Passion from the outside, as it were from the very edge of the crowd, that goes without saying. Our Lord was not content to die a painful death merely; he would die in ignominious circumstances. Imagine yourself a visitor to Jerusalem that day, with no knowledge of what was going on—how the demonstrations in front of Pilate's tribunal would have impressed you! A mob, though it be only a few hundreds of hired men, looks impressive; and there is a kind of herd-instinct in us which disposes us to think they must be right. If everybody wants to have a murderer reprieved, sooner than the Man they dislike so, depend upon it they must have good reason for such dislike. And so he goes to his death, in the company of two thieves; people stand round and ask, "Which is the Galilean? Oh, that one." A notice has been pinned up over his head; what does that say? THE KING OF THE JEWS—a joke, obviously, though perhaps not in the best of taste. And the whole point of the joke is to annoy the Jews by pointing to a broken Visionary as their King! "Is it nothing", asks the prophet, "to all you who pass by?" In heaven's name, why should it be anything? An innocent man sent to the gallows in first-century Judaea; there's nothing to be surprised about in that.

No, appearances were against him, if you didn't know the inside of the story. And if you did? Then you marched up and down in front of the Crucifix, mouthing out slogans. "He saved others, he cannot save himself. If he is the King of Israel, he has but to come down from the cross, here and now, and we will believe in him. He trusted in God; let God, if he favours him, succour him now; he told us, I am the Son of God." It was a kind of victory parade, a good way of blowing off steam before the sabbath. But at last you grew tired of it, and with one defiant "Let God succour him now", you turned to go home. And out of the darkness, as if it were an echo of your own taunt, came the sudden cry: "My God, my God, why hast thou forsaken me?"

Incredible, if our own ears had not witnessed it! He has recanted; he has owned himself in the wrong! The Gentiles who stood there could make nothing of the cry; they thought it was an appeal to Elijah. But everybody who understood the language of Palestine must have accepted it as an admission of defeat. And, worse than that, wherever this Gospel was preached in the whole world, those words would be a stumbling-block to the enquirer. "I don't understand", he would say, "about this Christ of yours. He seems to have abandoned his position in despair at the last moment. I don't wonder, after the barbarous way in which they had used him. But—can this be the Son of God?" So neglectful of appearances to the last, he would throw down that challenge to our faith and be content with the homage of such as would accept him still.

His martyrs in past ages have not been called upon to suffer such complete obscuration of fame. They faced death with expressions of undiminished hope, and won, at least, the applause of posterity. In our own time, unless the suspicions of a whole world are at fault, persecution has found a new weapon. It contrives so to work on the mental fibre of its victims, that they will sign and utter statements utterly at variance with their known opinions. "Ecce homo!" it cries, and produces for our inspection not a *man*, but a shrinking figure incapable of human actions. It seeks to discredit us in the eyes of our fellow Christians, to tarnish the fame of us which will go down to history. If those suspicions are well founded, a new chapter will have opened in the history of martyrdom. But still the disciple will not be above his Master, that Master who died commending his soul to God, yet with a phrase of dereliction on his lips.

One thing we were meant to see, written on the Crucifix as large as life, as large as death—that we must remit the judgement of all our action entirely to God. To do otherwise, to fortify ourselves in human opinion, is a kind of constructive idolatry. I am not thinking of that headstrong obstinacy which rejects all advice and then, finding the world critical, throws itself back upon God in a passion of hysterical self-righteousness. I am thinking of people who have to drag along, looking after difficult cases, relations of theirs, superiors of theirs, and get nothing but a scolding for their pains; I am thinking of people who honestly and humbly try to do good in the world, but, through some unconscious fault of manner, only succeed in making themselves unpopular. For these, there is no peace until they learn that only the divine award matters. "See how the eyes of servants are fixed on the hands of their masters, the eyes of a maid on the hand of her mistress! Our eyes, too, are fixed upon the Lord our God." It is from his grave and kindly judgement that we look for that final verdict of "Well done", which will make all earth's praises look so foolish, and all earth's prizes so trumpery.

XI

SIX STEPS TO THE CRUCIFIX

Our Lord Jesus Christ went to his death almost in silence—just a few necessary words to the commissars of the high priest, who arrested him; in the presence of the high priest, an obstinate refusal to plead, followed by an admission so curt that it was fatal; before Pilate, the same attitude of reserve, then a few cryptic answers, not likely to do his cause any good. He made the Way of the Cross without a word, as far as we know, for anybody, except the little group of women that bewailed him—no gesture, even, as far as we know, apart from that shake of the head with which he refused the offer of drugged wine. On the Cross, he spoke seven times, but with what economy! Twenty-eight words, perhaps, in the Aramaic. Almost throughout that tragedy, the chief Actor plays his part in dumb show. And till now, he has been so ready to answer our difficulties! Even when he used parables, under what homely veils he wrapped up eternal truth; and if we went to him and said, "Explain to us the parable", he was so patient with our thick wits. Now, he will leave us to puzzle it all out for ourselves, just when the sky above us grows dark, and faith is harder put to it than ever, just when we needed the reassuring accents of his voice! We crowd round, peering and pointing, doing our best to read the secret of it all; what does it mean, this ignominious end of a great mission? What does it mean, this sudden apostasy on the part of a nation so long disciplined, so greatly loved? What does it mean, this divine neglect of a Divine Victim? If he would only speak!

Well, we try and piece it together as best we can. I think you can say that there are six different levels from which men look at our Lord's Passion, and try to understand what it is about, some getting nearer than others to the whole truth of it. Shall we imagine the Crucifix as standing high above us, at the top of a flight of steps or platforms, and the human race in general as ranged upon those platforms, nearer or further off as it is given them to see more or less of the mystery? Only I think we shall find that even those who are on the highest step of all are not on a level with the foot of the Crucifix itself. The Crucifix itself stands on a plane too high for our intelligence; always there will be something imperfect, something lacking in our attempts to master it. Let us climb those six steps one by one; and, if you will, let us bend down and kiss each of those steps as we come to it, like the people who climb up the Holy Stair at Rome; at any level, even at the lowest, there is something here for poor bewildered humanity to adore.

On the lowest level of all, then, what does the spectator of Calvary say to himself? He shrugs his shoulders and comments, "Well, I suppose that is the way of the world! Here was a man who was too good for his generation; and his generation took the short way, and made an end of him." I doubt if there is a single human being who will not go as far as that with us, who will not pay that much tribute to the character of Jesus Christ. However low you rank him in the scale of human achievement, you will put him in the same class with Socrates. Socrates went about the world trying to make people *think*, trying to make people see that there must be a right and a wrong way of living. Every common thing, a saw or a spade or a shuttle, had a special use for which it was designed, and must be shaped in a particular way so that the purpose of it might be achieved. Man, therefore, and every individual man, must have a special use for which he was designed, and must be shaped in a particular way so that *his* purpose might be achieved. And the good people of Athens called him an atheist and made him drink poison. Five centuries later, Jesus of Nazareth came, and he taught, well, perhaps not exactly the same but the same *kind* of thing. He tried to persuade the Jews that the outside of things didn't matter, washing up cups and dishes and doing no work on Saturday; what mattered was the inside of things—being merciful to your neighbour, judging him charitably, trusting Providence, being sorry when you had done wrong. And the Jews crucified him. It is the way of the world.

Of the *world*; we mustn't go away saying, "Of course, Jews are like that." No, Jews and Gentiles are like that, the world is like that, and you and I are the world. All of us, the moment we take our eyes off the Crucifix, begin to make that mistake of thinking that it's the outside things which matter. No, I don't mean to discourage the washing of cups and dishes; that's all in the day's work. But think of all the shams you and I go in for; think of all the face-saving we do, instinctively, the moment we stop thinking about the Crucifix. Look at yourself for a moment; how quick you are to cover up your tracks, when you've made a fool of yourself; how anxious to make a good impression when you meet people; how ready to explain away your failures; how often you find yourself criticizing somebody you dislike, not for the reason which makes you dislike him, but for some quite different reason, hoping to get out of it that way! All shams, you see, all face-saving. Men loved darkness, rather than the light; we are truth-shy, all of us, Gentiles as well as Jews. And when somebody shows up the falseness in our scale of values, we hate it—as likely as not, hate him. That is how Socrates came to his end. On this lowest platform of all, we see the Crucifixion as the defeat of Truth in a world that loves its comfortable evasions. We cannot help being sorry about that; the only question is, whether we are going to treat it as inevitable, part of the natural order of things, or whether we shall try to do something, ourselves, about it.

Kiss that step, and go up one higher. The Passion of Jesus Christ is a shining example of heroism. It shows you a Man who holds principle dearer than his own convenience, dearer than life itself. Regulus, the Roman general, captured by the enemy, is sent back by the Carthaginians to negotiate peace and an exchange of prisoners. He is warned that it will be the worse for him if he does not succeed. He gets up in the senate and says, because he believes, that peace will be a bad thing for his country; let the prisoners remain prisoners; then he goes back to Carthage to die. Jesus of Nazareth is challenged, at his judgement, to say whether he is the Christ, the Son of the living God. He doesn't argue, doesn't qualify, doesn't temporize. He doesn't answer, as he might quite well have answered, "How should I know? This and that I have done; what do you think about it yourselves?" He says quite openly, "I am." When we read about such gestures of heroic courage, we are in two minds about it; there are moods in which our comment is, "More fool he." But we know, when we are saying that, how much we are belittled. It is because we are doubtful of our own heroic qualities, because we are not quite certain whether *we* should have the courage to speak out if we were put to the test, that we take refuge in cynicism: "More fool he; what good is done by such gestures, after all?" But at the heart of us, we admire. Even if we think the man was quite wrong, quite misguided, we cannot choose but admire. It comforts us with a more exalted view of our own poor human nature, that there should be human beings who can thus take a stand on principle, when they are alone and at the mercy of their enemies, when their loneliness and their helplessness make them look foolish.

You see, we are beginning to get into an atmosphere of mystery already. We are being taught to recognize that a particular course of action may be the best thing to do, may in a sense be the only thing to do, although it does not seem to produce any material advantage whatsoever. We are being taught to realize that man's sense of appreciation can rise higher than his own dull level of performance; you and I may not be very heroic souls, but if we see actions performed on the heroic level, we fall in love with them; we are stage-struck with an ideal. We are so very human; but there is something in us that answers, there is a bell that rings somewhere, at the challenge of the Divine.

I said, "Although it doesn't seem to produce any material advantage whatever"; but is that true, after all, of any great gesture made by a man of principle in defence of his principles? We all know the old saying that "the blood of the martyrs is the seed of the Church", and how often that has been proved true; how often the death of some great public figure has proved to be a living inspiration! I should think that when a fanatic, let us hope, a lunatic, put an end to Gandhi's life, all he did was to lay the foundation of a Gandhi legend. If there is any hope at all of peace and good government for the puzzled millions of India, I should think it lies in the memory of a man who did, maybe, much good and much harm in his life-time, but now, in his death, stands for a symbol of mutual understanding, mutual toleration. Do what we will, say what we will, there is something about violent death which sets the seal, for good or ill, on a man's life; and if he died trying to do good, his memory becomes a talisman.

And that is our third step on the approach to Calvary. Jesus of Nazareth claims homage, even from millions of people who do not believe that he was God, because his death sealed, unmistakably, the life he had lived. To be sure, mankind has a short memory and can live down even the death of a hero. But there is something about the story of Calvary, which has never failed, which, faith and experience alike proclaim it, *will* never fail to arrest the attention, and to arouse the sympathy, of the human heart. Pull down the churches, massacre the priests, forbid the teaching of religion, but still, as long as there is a Bible left in the world, you have to reckon with the influence of Jesus of Nazareth. Lifted up, he draws men to him with a magnetism which all the changing fashions of human thought cannot neutralize. Buried in the ground, this grain of wheat will take life and flourish anew.

But when we have said that, we haven't said everything. We have spoken of the hero as if he were necessarily a man of principle, firmly convinced that he is right over some one particular point and prepared to face death on behalf of that conviction. Is that all we mean by a hero? Does it not make him rather inhuman, if we think of him as interested exclusively in the rights and wrongs of a particular case, and not at all in the lives of his fellow men? I think we shall all agree that in the shining annals of history those heroes rank highest, of whom it can be said that they lived, and often that they died, for others. And so we mount on to the fourth step of our ascent. We shall get a little nearer the heart of Calvary when we see the Victim of it in that light, when we have given a little thought to the motto which he inscribed on the threshold of Gethsemani: "This is the greatest love a man can show, that he should lay down his life for his friends."

A man's death is never so splendid, as when you can say, "He died that others might live." On Scott's last expedition—we all know the story—there was one of his companions, Oates, who knew that he was being a drag on the rest of the party; without him, their rations would last longer, and they would have more chance of getting home in safety. He walked out into the snow, and was never seen again. Every generous instinct in our natures tells us to see the situation as it must have appeared to Oates himself—a chance of doing the more difficult thing, and making things more easy for other people. Jesus of Nazareth—I think Saint John means us to see that, although he doesn't draw much attention to it—gave himself up deliberately into his enemies' power because he wanted to save his friends. "If I am the man you are looking for," he says to the Temple guard, "let these others go free." The words had, it is clearly implied, a mystical significance. They referred, really, to all those millions of souls, yours and mine, please God, which were to be ransomed for ever by the doings of that night. But their immediate application was something simpler; the representatives of law and order may let the gang disperse, now that the Ringleader has given himself up. On this fourth level of approach, it is enough for us to know *that*; Jesus Christ died, that others might live.

So far, we have been thinking of our Lord's death merely as a death; from these lower levels of contemplation, we have not been free to observe the details of it. Nor had we any need to; for all the purposes we have hitherto been considering, it is enough that a man should die; we do not stop to enquire whether he died thus or thus, whether he died suddenly or painlessly. But when we reach the fifth step of our upward journey, we familiarize ourselves with the grim details of the Passion; it is not merely a death, it is a pageant of suffering. To some of us, the thought of great pain, of great cruelty, is one from which the mind shrinks away in a kind of nervous revolt; we cannot read in the newspapers, the long and harrowing descriptions they give of concentration camps; it suffices us to feel indignation, without entering into the ghastly circumstances of it all. May it not be the same with our Lord's Passion? Must we follow it step by step—the night of dismay, the arrest, the mock trial, the buffeting, the scourging, the Crown, the mockery, the Via Dolorosa, the nails, the Cross, the faintness, the dereliction, the thirst? Can we not take it as read?

Not quite, I think, and for this reason. Suffering is the punishment for sin; and our sins are many and of long duration; we must watch them being expiated on the Cross by many sufferings, by sufferings that last on and on. We shall not feel the true nature of our sins without that. On this fifth platform of our ascent, you see, we go one stage further; we see Jesus of Nazareth not merely crucified for others, but crucified for the sins of others. Where shall we find any parallel to that? An imperfect one, perhaps, in the Old Testament. The book of Job is all about the sufferings of an innocent man; that is the whole argument of it. But in his case it is represented as a test of faith; it was not till the full revelation came to us in the Person of our Lord that we were allowed to see the whole truth about sin and suffering. Not till then were we allowed to see that the innocent may suffer, taking upon himself, by a voluntary welcome, the sins of the guilty.

Is that the best we can do? To represent the whole doctrine of our redemption in terms of a debt incurred, and a debt paid? There is something a little mathematical, I had almost said, something a little commercial, about such a way of talking. It may appeal to us as theologians; it does not satisfy our hearts. Let us rather mount up to the sixth stage of the ascent, and catch, I will not say a different picture of the truth, but a different angle on the truth. If Jesus

Christ suffered, it was surely because, in this imperfect world, love cannot express itself except in terms of suffering; and the greatness of our Lord's sufferings is the measure of his love. That lesson, I think, you can learn if you will read the life of any one of his saints; that is the thread which binds together the infinitely various nosegay of their sanctity; suffering, to them, is the air which love breathes, and to be without suffering, if you love our Lord as much as that, is to be stifled for want of air. Take Saint Francis, if you will, for your type here; see what reward was given him at the end of a life so spent for God! Not the impress of our Lord's Crown in heaven, but the impress, on hands and feet, of our Lord's sufferings; as a great privilege, just for that last bit of his life, Francis may bleed with Christ.

I suspect that all we have said about the meaning of the Passion is about as much like what the Passion *really* means, as a school-boy's essay on atomic physics is like atomic physics. Not wrong as far as it goes, but only an adumbration of the truth.

You see, the Passion is a mystery. We can tell ourselves that a world like ours was bound to reject Jesus Christ, as it rejected Socrates. We can admire his lonely courage, like that of Regulus; watch his death becoming, like the death of Gandhi, an inspiration to his followers. We can see him giving his life for others, like Oates the explorer; suffering, like Job, although he had no sin to atone for; suffering, like Saint Francis and all those other saints of his, because suffering is the native language of love. But all those are only glimpses which obscure the central truth, just as the high lights on the facets of a diamond make it impossible to see the diamond. The Passion is a mystery.

And it is meant to be, because it is meant to call out in us the quality of faith. It is the very nature of faith to thrive on mystery. You and I have got to see in the story of Calvary something which is to us incomprehensible at every turn—Omnipotence defeated, the death of the Eternal, the sufferings of the Impassible, the punishment of the All-holy. In the crevices of that bare rock our faith is to take root and grow. We shall need faith, you and I, in a world where the cause of Christ has enemies so numerous and so powerful, in a world that threatens to abolish the very vocabulary of religion. And we shall have strength to conquer, not in spite of the fact but because of the fact, that the life of our crucified Master ended, not in a victory, but in a defeat.

He told us so little, when he went out to die; he tells us so little, even now. He doesn't want us to understand; he wants us to believe.

XII

THE PASSION AS OUR LORD SAW IT

You do not, as a rule, go through a retreat without having a meditation on our Lord's Passion. Why is that? After all, it is not quite what you have expected. Because the whole idea of a retreat is that you should concentrate your attention on yourself. You ask why God made *you*; you reflect on the shortness of life, on the eternity that awaits *you* after death, on *your* sins, on the vocation God has for *you* in the world, and so on—it is all about *you*. But quite suddenly, in the middle, we stop thinking about ourselves and start thinking about our Lord instead; why is that? I think it can be explained by a very simple parable. When you have a lot of people singing without any organ accompaniment, there is a constant tendency for the note to drop all the time; it gets lower and lower as it goes on. And therefore, when the choir isn't accustomed to singing without accompaniment, every now and then the choir-master, who has a pitch-pipe concealed on his person, gives a little *toot* in the background, to remind them of the higher note which they ought to be taking, and aren't.

And, you see, we are rather like that. We go on living from day to day without thinking much about how we are living, or what we are here for, or whether the things that chiefly interest us are really worth living for; and we get accustomed to our sins and feel vaguely that it is a pity we go on committing them, but after all, there doesn't seem to be much chance of our stopping; and our prayers get very languid and washed out, and we think of very little except our food and our amusements—do you see what I mean? All the time, the note on which our lives are lived is dropping, dropping, till it's ready to die away into our boots, and *we don't notice*, just as the choir doesn't notice when the note drops. So we want that sudden little *toot* of the pitch-pipe, to pull us together and screw the note of our lives up again. And the pitch-pipe we use, when we go into retreat, is meditation on our Lord's Passion. We look for a moment at human life as he lived it, and the values of human life as he saw them; and we see that we were all wrong and start, please God, living our lives afresh, strung up to a higher pitch than before.

Now, when you want to meditate on our Lord's Passion, the ordinary thing to do is to try and imagine yourself as present among the spectators who witnessed the various stages of it. You picture yourself as one of the apostles at the Last Supper, when our Lord said one of them would betray him and they didn't know which; as one of the three who fell asleep in the garden; as one of the bystanders who saw our Lord arrested, who heard Saint Peter deny him three times in the judgement hall; as one of the soldiers who brought him before Pilate; as one of the crowd which shouted for his death and watched him while he hung on Calvary. You place yourself among the spectators and imagine yourself looking at our Lord, watching the expression on his face, listening to those few, but momentous words he utters. But it is possible, by the way of a change, to approach the same subject from a different angle. How would it be if we put ourselves, just for a few minutes, in our Lord's place, and tried to follow the story of Calvary as it was seen by his eyes? Of course, it is a rather daring thing to do, and we can only do it very imperfectly. He was God as well as man, and it isn't likely that you and I would be able to read his thoughts. He could read the future as you and I can't read it, he could read the secrets of other men's hearts, as you and I can't, and his will was perfectly submitted, all the time, to his heavenly Father's will, as, alas, your wills and mine aren't. But, making allowances, as we go, for all that stupendous difference between ourselves and him, we can, perhaps, get some sort of inkling of how it all looked, of what it all felt like, from the point of view of one person who was the Hero of it all and the Victim of it all, our Lord Jesus Christ himself.

He is kneeling there, in the half-darkness, among the olive-trees in Gethsemani. He is thinking about dying, about dying a very painful death; he is human, you see, and there is something about the thought of death which casts a chill over the bravest spirit; he wants to make his soul. But he is thinking also about Judas, who is going to betray him, about the men who will condemn him to death. You know how the thought of treachery, the thought of great cruelty, makes us feel sick when we hear about it, even you and me; what must that thought have been like to our Lord, who was holiness itself? No, it must not happen; somehow it must be prevented, this perversion of human justice! And yet, if they turn aside from that guilty purpose of theirs, how is the Christ to suffer, how is man to be redeemed? "Father, your will be done, not mine." The growing darkness, the loneliness, begin to weigh upon his spirits; he goes to look for his disciples, and finds them asleep. He knows they are tired; there are excuses for them. But he sees, don't you think, all down the centuries the picture of those friends of his who will fall asleep at their post; how many Christians there will be who will indulge their weaknesses, who will forget to watch, and be surprised by sudden temptation. Yes, his human friends are asleep, but when he goes back to his post to pray again, a figure is standing there beside him; he recognizes it for one of those bright angels who worship in his Father's presence. While earth sleeps, heaven watches; he is not alone in his prayer.

A light flickers down there among the olive-trees; there is a tramp of feet; it is the signal for his arrest. He wakes the friends who have fallen asleep, and stands there ready to meet the friend who does not sleep, but hastens to betray him to the Jews. And now he feels the touch of Judas' kiss on his cheek, those cold and trembling lips. He has much to suffer to-night, but perhaps, for his own feelings, that kiss was the worst heart-ache, the most bitter profanation of all. He thinks of all the treacheries there will be that will bring back the name of Judas to men's minds; he thinks of his priests who will play him false, of the sacrilegious Communions by which his presence will be profaned—well, that is over; they are binding him now; he prefers the feel of the ropes about his wrists. Force has triumphed; so, through history, superior force will triumph, again and again; truth and justice will be led away bound, and God will not interfere. His friends will be scandalized when they see that happen, just as they are being scandalized now as they see him led away unresisting; see, they have taken to their heels in the darkness! That, too, will happen again and again; the rulers of his Church will fail in courage; his followers—how many of them!—will play him false, will let the truth go, through human respect.

He knows where they are taking him; it will be Annas' house first, then Caiphas'. He looks round him in the judgement hall at the faces of his enemies. Each of them, from the high priest downwards, is trying to put on an air of extreme impartiality, of complete open-mindedness; each tries to look shocked as the witnesses depose their evidence—these witnesses they themselves have suborned! He will be silent, all through this perversion of justice, as God himself is silent when men, his creatures, pervert justice, that justice which is himself. Meanwhile, remember, our Lord's thoughts are not entirely concentrated on his judges, on what the witnesses are saying. He is looking at a corner of the court over yonder, where the serving-men are sitting over a fire. You can see their shadows reflected on the wall, and the features of one are familiar; Simon Peter is sitting there among them. You can see what they are talking about; they keep on looking round at him, all except Peter; they ply Peter with questions, and you can see the shake of his head, hear his voice raised in vigorous disagreement. So it goes on, until at last the argument grows hot; there are angry gestures; Peter's voice rises in violent imprecation. And the Lord turned and looked at Peter. In that look of his was all the gentle reproach with which he still looks at you and me when we trust too much in our own strength, presume on grace, and so fail him in the hour of trial; we shall see it for ourselves, one day.

He turns back, now, to answer the high priest's question. Yes, he is the Son of God; they will know that, he tells them, when he comes again in judgement. And now the faces of his judges drop the mask they wore; they gnash their teeth, shake their fists at him, cry out, with savage delight, for the death sentence. Quite suddenly, a bandage is put round his eyes, a welcome screen between him and the faces of his enemies. A blow falls on his cheek, first from one side, then from the other; "Prophesy, thou Christ, who is it that smote thee?" He doesn't answer their taunts, but he thinks, instead, of all the taunts his Church will have to undergo, century after century, how man's insolence will challenge it with its powerlessness to help itself, its powerlessness to save.

He is led away again; the chill air of the night strikes him; when the bandage is taken away, he finds himself in the darkness of the streets. There is no doubt where he is going; they are taking him off to the Roman governor. He stands, before long, facing a new tribunal; the looks of this one are quite different. There is no hatred, open or concealed, in the faces that meet him here; only surprise and—boredom. Pilate and his men sit there wondering how on earth these Jews manage to get so excited over their obscure religious controversies. After all, what is truth? What does it matter, if somebody chooses to call himself the Son of God? Why not let him go his own way? Does it comfort our Lord, to read thoughts like that in the faces of those who sit opposite him? I'm afraid not. It makes him think of all those people down the centuries who will reject him, reject his message, because they are simply indifferent to the truth, because they don't care whether God became man or not. There are so many practical things to be done; there is no time to go into these questions.

That is the atmosphere of Pilate's judgement hall; for half an hour or so, it may be, our Lord gets a respite from it. He is taken across to another building close by, to be questioned by King Herod. This is a very different affair; Herod has long been wanting to see our Lord, half-hoping, half-fearing, that it may be John the Baptist, the man he himself beheaded, come back to life. Anyhow, there are these stories about miracles; good, we shall see a miracle. What is written large on the dissolute features of Herod is curiosity, superstitious curiosity. Our Lord sees that; and perhaps he thinks how, all down the ages, there will be souls that will fail to respond to his message because it doesn't do enough to gratify their inquisitiveness; because it is a religion, and they wanted magic—souls, like Herod, too enquiring, and souls, like Pilate, not enquiring enough; our Lord thinks sadly how many there will be who will be brought into close touch with his message, who will have every opportunity of looking into it, and will make nothing of it all the same.

At last the travesty of justice is over. Our Lord is scourged by the soldiers, is treated with mock reverence, crowned as a king. The thorns hurt his forehead, but I don't think he minds all this mockery very much; they are only savage creatures, after all. So he is twice led out before the multitude, and the crowd he can see there surging beneath cries out, in spite of protests from Pilate, to have him crucified. The mob—he thinks how hopelessly fickle it is, the mob that shouted "Hosanna" five days back and is shouting "Crucify him!" now. This mob, and every other mob; he thinks of the terrible weakness human creatures show when they are packed together like that, how they lose their individuality, and join in the popular cry simply because it is the popular cry, not one of them really asking himself whether that is what he wants or not. And he thinks of the men behind that crowd, who have roused its passions, who have set it in motion; the terrible responsibility that will rest, all down the ages, with the men who know how to manage a crowd and teach it to do their bidding.

Then he is taken into the soldiers' quarters again. The first sight which meets his eyes there is a couple of rough planks, the shorter of them nailed across the longer one. A soldier shows him how he is to carry them. Our Lord must have felt, I think, like a priest when he first takes up the sacred vessels to say Mass; this is what he has lived for. So they start out on that painful journey to the place of death. How long do you imagine the Via Dolorosa to have been? One thinks of it, somehow, as a kind of pilgrimage; really, it was only a thousand paces or so; but they will have gone slowly through the narrow, tortuous streets of the crowded city. Our Lord is bending down, under his Cross; he only sees the faces of the bystanders now and again, where some group of women, perhaps, has been driven back into a corner to let the cortège pass by. He sees them lamenting for him; and the sight suggests to his mind the day, only forty years later, when the Roman armies will have closed round the city, and nothing but lamentation will ring through these streets. "Daughters of Jerusalem, do not weep for me, but for yourselves and your children." All the tragedies of innocent lives taken, and unoffending homes wrecked, for the sake of causes which ordinary citizens can hardly understand, opens up to him in the long vista of the future, and he turns from his own sufferings to compassionate theirs.

They pass under the city gate; a visitor to Jerusalem, waiting to let them pass, is roughly accosted by the soldiers, who tell him to help carry the Cross. In him, in Simon of Cyrene, our Lord rejoices to see the figure of all those servants of his who will be inspired to great deeds and splendid mortifications by the thought that they are doing just this. So aided, he finishes the rest of the journey without much difficulty; it was not such a great distance, after all. There is a halt here and a rest; the soldiers, less rough in their manner now that the troubles of the journey are over, offer him the drugged wine which the charity of kindly women has supplied, to deaden the pain of crucifixion. No, that must not happen; he must drink the cup of suffering his Father has sent him, drink it fasting. He is stripped and nailed down; the Cross is lifted up. Now he has a wider view than he had during the rest of his Passion; so far, there has always been a ring of faces round him; now he can look down from a height at the city, the faithless city that has so often refused his invitations and has now disowned him; he can look up at the sky, grey already with the unnatural twilight that heralds an eclipse of the sun. He looks down, in imagination, not only at the city but at the world that lies beyond it, the nations whom his Father has given him to be his possession. People far away, in remote islands like Britain, will hear the story of this day's work and will turn to him with faith and repentance. There are only two faces, now, on his own level—the hateful face of the Impenitent Thief, blaspheming to the last, and the appealing eyes of Dismas, as he asks mercy from a King, counts, not without justice, on his royal gift of remembering faces.

Close underneath—it does not much matter what is happening close underneath. He hears the rattle of the soldiers' dice-box; let them play; they do not know, after all, what it is they are doing. Worse than their indifference are the mocking looks of his enemies; so it will always be, down the centuries; all the love he squanders on some of his fellow men will only harden their hearts. But stay, there is something else. Down there, his Mother and his friend—some word must be said for their comfort. They are all he has; their destinies must be knit together, as his final legacy to the Church. Then he can turn away his thoughts from earth to heaven.

He turns his thoughts to heaven, to find heaven, somehow, shut against them. We dare not guess what his feelings were when he cried out, "My God, my God, why hast thou forsaken me?"; the greatest of contemplatives have only caught some echo of that mysterious dereliction which assailed the fortress of a human soul when God hung upon the Cross God-forsaken. At least we can guess this, that when he faced that conflict he meant to hallow for us, and to lighten for us, all the worst times you and I will ever have to go through. The cloud passed from him, it would seem, when he had only a few more minutes to live. He lived to accept a draught of wine from one of his executioners—thought, perhaps, as he did so, of all those acts of charity which would be done in his name, often by men and women who had scarcely heard of it. Then, conscious that he had paid the price in full, he resigned, by a deliberate act, his human spirit, abandoned it, with utter confidence, into his Father's hands. The sabbath day was coming; he would rest from his labours.

So, I think, the world must have looked to the eyes of its Redeemer during those last eighteen hours before they closed in death. You and I have each of us a different world-picture, moulded by our individual circumstances, coloured by our individual temperaments. If we would learn to face our own problems, to achieve our own destinies, we must ask grace to see the world as he saw it, with that same unity of purpose, with that same abandonment of ourselves, and all that belongs to us, and all that is to become of us, to the good pleasure of a divine and an over-ruling will. We have been trying to put ourselves in the Heart of Jesus Christ. Let us ask God to put Jesus Christ into your heart and mine, so that it may be Christ living in us, as long as we live, Christ dying in us, when we come to die.

XIII

THE PROBLEM OF SUFFERING

The prophet Isaiah, in the great passage in which he foretells most clearly the death and Passion of our Lord Jesus Christ, makes use of one phrase in particular which gives the key to any right Christian understanding of the whole story—I mean the phrase "he was offered because he willed it". From first to last, you have to remember, there is one Accomplice who co-operates more effectively with the plans of our Lord's persecutors than any other, and that is our Lord himself.

It is extraordinary how that comes out, even if you think of our Lord's actions, at the time of his betrayal and his judgement, merely as human actions. Those scholars who approach the story of the Gospels with the assumption that our Lord was only a man, and that the significance of his death was merely the significance which attaches to the death of a great religious thinker or a great moral reformer, are ludicrously unsuccessful when they try to find any reason why our Lord was put to death at all. Consider: Jerusalem was full of our Lord's friends and partisans at the time of the feast. He could have been perfectly safe if he had been content to sleep the Thursday night away from Jerusalem; and there was nothing to prevent him from doing so; Thursday was not the actual day of the feast. Instead, he remained in Jerusalem and laid himself open to an attack by night. He knew that Judas was going to betray him—knew, therefore, that it would be safest to avoid the places which were his familiar walks; instead, he went straight out to Gethsemani, as if he had had an appointment with Judas there. He took swords with him, but he would not allow them to be used in his defence. He spent the evening praying that he might be spared from the fate which he foresaw; but if he foresaw it and wanted to escape it, why did he not leave Gethsemani and take refuge in the friendly darkness? At his trial it is the same; before the high priest, where silence might have saved him, he speaks; before Pilate, where he had only to speak, he remains silent. More than once he had refused to let his fellow-countrymen make a king of him; now, when he is bound hand and foot before the Roman governor, he will not disown the royal title. There is only one explanation of it; he wants to die.

But of course we know that that isn't all; we know that he did not merely behave, as man, in such a way as to prejudice his chances of reprieve; he was, all the time, Omnipotent God, and could order the course of things as he would. Twelve legions of angels, he told Saint Peter, were ready to spring to his defence if he had willed it; they stand there, hand on scabbard, and he waves them back. How easily the story might have fallen out otherwise! How easily, for example, Pilate might have been overpersuaded by his wife's message and have insisted on crucifying Barabbas after all! But no, it was part of God's providential design for our salvation that everything should fall out exactly as it did. God wanted to die.

Not that his death was necessary, remember, for our redemption. Every prayer he offered, every sigh he uttered, every moment he lived on earth had, of itself, an infinite satisfactory value which was enough, since he was God, to atone for the sins of the world. He could have accomplished the salvation of the world even if he had seen fit to ascend to his Father from his cradle at Bethlehem. But he wouldn't do that; he would pay the price in full. He would not merely come to earth, but live thirty-three years on earth; not merely live here, but toil, hunger, thirst, feel weariness; not only that, but he would be persecuted and hunted to his death; not merely die, but die with every circumstance of ignominy, after experiencing the most acute forms of bodily torment. The reparation was not in proportion to the fault; grace abounded; he became man to make atonement for us, but having become man, he was not content merely to make atonement, he would make it in full.

What was the meaning of that? It is not for us to expect that we should be able to understand, in detail, the counsels of God's Wisdom, even where they are so intimately concerned with ourselves. But we can try to represent to ourselves, according to our human measure, something of what those counsels were meant to achieve. In the first place, it was fitting that the Son of God should die, because he came to deliver us from that sentence of death which was the punishment for our sins. In order to assure us of the hope of a blessed immortality, he challenged death in his own Person—underwent its sentence and raised himself from the tomb.

And again, it was fitting that the Son of God should choose a life of hardship and of toil when he came to earth, if only so that he might teach us a lesson of generosity. He was going to demand of his followers a spirit of unquestioning self-sacrifice; those who were nearest to him and highest in his favour would find the greatest demands made on them, and need the greatest heroism to meet them. Fitting, therefore, that our Captain should himself share the difficulties which his soldiers would have to contend with; he does not ask, Can you drink of the chalice of suffering I will mingle for you?—he asks, Can you drink of the chalice of suffering which I drink of? Our Lord would not demand that we should show our love for him in that way, without first showing us in that way his Love for us. That we can understand; he was not content merely to be our Ransom, he would be our Model.

But is even that a full explanation? After all, the first martyr who was called upon to testify his loyalty by death, Saint Stephen, was killed by stoning. There was a time, if you remember, when our Lord's enemies took up stones to kill him, but he escaped and passed through the midst of them. He came to die, but he would not die by any martyrdom that was speedy and direct; he reserved himself for the scourging, and the Crown of Thorns, and the Cross with its long agony of dissolution. He did not merely desire death, he did not merely desire hardship and poverty, he desired suffering. You may almost say that the very word "passion" acquired for the first time, when it was applied to our Lord, a positive meaning. To "suffer", after all, in Greek or in Latin, merely means "to have something done to you"; passion is merely the opposite of action. But our Lord has so dignified the very notion of suffering that it has taken on a kind of active force; to suffer is to *do* something, since *he* came to earth and made suffering the crown and the ambition of his career. Why is that? Why did he want that? Surely because, next to the mystery of death itself, the most baffling mystery of human life is the existence, the omnipresence, the distribution of suffering. And he wanted, not indeed to explain that mystery in full; probably our minds in this present state of our knowledge are not capable of understanding it in full; but he wanted to give us some clue which would help us to unravel it a little, some window of light which would penetrate, though it might not dispel, the darkness which hung and still hangs over our mortal lot.

Man has been trying to understand pain almost as long as he has experienced it. One thing seems clear about it; it is an ineradicable conviction of the human mind that pain is, somehow, the appropriate retribution for wrong-doing; the man who has done evil must suffer evil. Sometimes we can trace without difficulty a direct connexion between the two, as when disease follows upon the abuse of our physical powers, or when the selfishness of a depraved nature brings with it its own punishment of jealousy, heartbreak, and remorse. And it was natural for theology, in its earliest stages, to assume that this principle held good everywhere—that any kind of harm or misfortune that befell a man was a punishment exactly proportioned to his sins. You will find the heathen authors full of that idea, complicated slightly by the notion that a man might be punished for the sins of his fathers, which was also familiar to Jewish thought. "Did this man sin, or his parents, that he was born blind?"—the question is still being asked, you see, in our Lord's time.

There is one book of the Old Testament which is concerned entirely with the problem of suffering, and carries it a stage further; I mean the book of Job. The situation there is, of course, that Job has lost all his property, has been overwhelmed with grief by the death of his sons and daughters, and has himself been smitten with a painful disease; his friends, therefore, assume that he must have offended God, and urge him to make confession of his sin. But Job has not done anything to deserve these misfortunes; that is the point of the story. Why, then, have they been allowed to befall him? The answer, so far as an answer is given, is this. If happiness and prosperity were exactly proportioned to our deserts in this world, how should we ever be certain that our neighbours, or indeed that we ourselves, were serving God out of love for him or reverence for him, and not simply because we found it paid? "Doth Job serve God for nought?" is Satan's question; and he can only be proved wrong when Job loses all the material advantages he enjoyed and is found still submissive, still confident in God's mercy, in the midst of his misfortune. Suffering has this office at least, that it winnows the chaff from the wheat, shows up the false devotion that is merely cupboard-love, and makes true devotion shine all the brighter, like gold in the furnace.

That is an answer, but of course it is only a partial one. Granted that our love of God can only be *proved* by suffering, why is it necessary that it should be proved at all, or for whose benefit is the proof needed? And even if you go further and say—what is true as a matter of observation—that in some cases suffering appears not only to exhibit strength in the character of the person who undergoes it, but actually to put a strength there which was not there before; even if you claim that suffering not merely reveals the saint but makes the saint, our restless intellect might still ask why, in God's Providence, that hard discipline should be necessary—why he, who is all-powerful and all-wise, could not have devised some other way of perfecting us, without all this pain and suffering which is a scandal and a cause of blasphemy instead to so many others.

The story of Calvary, then, takes us still further. Jesus Christ suffered; was that because Jesus Christ had sinned? The very thought is profane. Jesus Christ suffered; was that because it was necessary to prove that his love of God was disinterested? He, who was himself Incarnate God, and had become man to redeem us, was proof necessary that his was no mercenary love? Jesus Christ suffered; was that because suffering was needed to perfect his character? But his character was already perfect; he had not even inherited from his Mother the taint of our common sinfulness; he was all purity, all unselfishness. Why then, if he suffered, there must be some further value in suffering still unguessed at. He chose suffering; he embraced it. Not that it was a good thing in itself; of its nature suffering is an evil, and he showed us that when he prayed in the garden to be delivered from the chalice of his Passion. But when it came to him, he carried it like a banner. He would not even accept the wine mingled with myrrh which they offered him, charitably, when they nailed him to the Cross. He would drink his cup to the dregs, relish the flavour of it—no ache, no throb of crucifixion, but had, somehow, a meaning and a value for him.

Surely he wanted us to see this—that all suffering is the expiation of sin, involves sin, but that he who commits the sin is not necessarily he who suffers for it. He prayed that the chalice might pass from him, because it came to him tainted with human sin, the result of human sin, not his own. It involved the treachery of Judas, the cowardice of Peter, the malice of the priests, the cynical injustice of Pilate, the brutality of the soldiers. Antecedently, therefore, he hated it, as he hated all the sins of all the whole world for which, nevertheless, he was prepared to suffer. But positing the existence of sin which needed to be expiated, he took that expiation upon himself as a privilege and a prize; no Crown was worthy of the second Adam except one woven of thorns—the thorns which the first Adam's transgression had sown in the earthly Paradise.

And here is another curious point about the history of the Passion which has never, I think, puzzled the critics of the Gospel as much as it ought to have puzzled them—our Lord, while he does not spare himself pain, does not even seem to spare pain to others. That he should want to go away into a quiet place while he nerves himself for the ordeal that lies before him is natural enough; but why does he want to take three of his friends to share the circumstances of his Agony? Why does he reproach them when he finds them asleep, as if he wanted them to be conscious of every tide of feeling that passes over him? Surely it is the instinct of a brave man to go away by himself, to keep out of sight of his friends for fear that he may communicate his own distress to others. In the same way, although (as I have said) he is anxious to savour the bitterness of his Passion to the full, our Lord allows Simon of Cyrene to help in carrying his Cross; why is that? And, at the Crucifixion itself, he will allow our Blessed Lady to be present, and to witness the cruel undoing of the Body she brought into the world—why is that? Why is it that he will not keep his sufferings to himself?

He will not keep his sufferings to himself, because that would be avarice in one who was so prodigal of pain. As he covets suffering for himself, so he will allow his best friends to share it; their watchfulness, their sighs, their tears shall be privileged to co-operate with him in the work of the world's redemption—and hers, most of all, who alone was privileged to co-operate in the work of the Incarnation. She is allowed to feel the sword of martyrdom, because for her as for him suffering is something to be desired and to be embraced.

> Before her eyes,
> Her, and the whole world's joys,
> Hanging all torn she sees, and in his woes
> And pains, her pangs and throes;
> While with a faithful, mutual flood
> Her eyes bleed tears, his wounds weep blood.

She too was sinless; she too had deserved nothing of Eve's curse; in her, then, as in him, the mystery of suffering is made plain to us—she accepts it, not for herself but for us.

The saints of Christendom in every age have understood that lesson. To be sure, they had sins of their own to make reparation for, and in their humility they did not dare to think of their sufferings as out of proportion to their deserts. But in uniting those sufferings as they did with the Passion of Christ they gave a more telling force and a wider significance. "In this mortal frame of mine", writes Saint Paul, "I help to pay off the debt which the afflictions of Christ leave still to be paid, for the sake of his body, the Church"—still to be paid, not in the sense that the satisfaction made once for all on Calvary was incomplete, but in the sense that those pains lavished for us leave us under an honourable obligation to discharge all we can of them, on our own behalf and on behalf of a guilty humanity. That solidarity which our Lord established among his creatures, by making himself the Head of a redeemed race, is not sufficiently appreciated until we learn to feel the sins of all Christ's members as in some sense our own, claiming our part in the reparation that is due for them.

That, then, is the light which our Lord's Passion throws on the mystery of suffering. It does not explain everything; it does not tell us, for example, why it is that the dumb animals suffer, although they have no moral will by which they can identify themselves with a divine purpose, no eternity in which they can be rewarded. But it gives us something better than a merely intellectual explanation; it gives us an inspiration by which we ourselves, if we try to follow our Lord in the way of love, can accept suffering, an attitude with which to meet it. It consoles us for what is a matter of common experience—that those souls who are closest to God seem to suffer not less, but more than the generality of his creatures. That becomes clear when we remember that their appetite for suffering is greater, and demands more to satisfy it. For ourselves, let us fear a life which is too full of comforts and of consolations, lest it should prove an unsanctified life and leave us with all the more sins to expiate in Purgatory. And when suffering comes to us, in body or in mind, as it must come to all of us, let us not profane it by asking "What have *I* done to deserve *this*?" We are helping to pay the debt due for the world's sins. Let us unite it with our Lord's Agony and Passion, thanking him that he has deigned so to take us into his own fellowship, so to honour us with the royal dignity of his Cross.

XIV

THE WAY OF LOVE

Our Lord says, "If any man has a mind to come my way, let him take up his cross and follow me." I want you to set before your minds the picture of a mournful procession, a procession of three men, each of whom carries a cross. We do not know in what order they marched, but one of them will be the thief who afterwards died, so far as we know, impenitent; one of them will be Saint Dismas, who turned back to God in his agony and was received that same day into Paradise; the third is our Lord himself. Our Lord is not content to remain still and suffer at the hands of others; he will undertake one last exhausting labour on our behalf, shoulder the instrument of his Agony. He who was born of a carpenter's wife will be a Carpenter to the end.

I don't think it is altogether fanciful to suggest that each of those three is bearing his cross in a different spirit, and that they typify, severally, the three different ways in which it is possible for a man to bear the yoke which God lays upon all of us—I mean, the yoke of the moral law, so ungracious to the indolence and peevishness of our fallen nature. You may bear it protestingly, in a spirit of rebellion; you may bear it grudgingly, in a spirit of acquiescence; or you may bear it joyfully, in a spirit of love.

The Impenitent Thief—so we call him, though it is not for us to know in what dispositions of mind his death agony found him—marches there, I take it, in resentful protest. Society, he tells himself, is his enemy, as it is always the enemy of the under-dog. He has robbed men of riches to which they had no real right, and society, protecting the rich as always, has turned against him. He carries the yoke because he must—the soldiers are there with their cruel thongs to see that he does. He carries the yoke because he must; if only he could see his chance, he would swing round the cross and bring it down on the head of the centurion, trusting to luck to get clear in the confusion that followed. And here is this pretended Prophet from Galilee, who claims to be able to do miracles; what a contemptible Slave he must be, if those stories are true, to go on meekly to his death instead of delivering himself by some feat of conjuring! He curses the day he was born, and the sunlight, and the Roman governor and all the legal system of Rome.

Dismas, as far as we know, did not feel the call of grace till later; at first, it seems possible, he too hurled taunts at his innocent fellow-prisoner. But we may perhaps be allowed to conjecture that even then, even as he shared the Via Dolorosa, he had some better feelings about his situation, "and we indeed justly"—so he was to say, an hour or two later; he has been thinking, evidently, and perhaps those thoughts came to him as he carried his cross. It is hard (he reflects) that it should have come to this. If only I had stuck to an honest way of living, instead of getting into bad company! I would give a lot to be able to go to my death an innocent man, like that Galilean. There's no use, anyhow, in complaining; I must shoulder this cross, because it's all that I have deserved. There must be laws, and it's no good having laws without punishments; I will jog along as best I may, grateful at least that I haven't got to undertake the journey after a scourging, like that other. It will all be over before long; that's one comfort.

And the third cross-bearer? Let us put ourselves in his place, as far as reverence will allow it, and imagine what thoughts were his, as he trod the same road under the same burden.

> Blessed above all the trees of the forest be these rough planks I take on my shoulders, the balance on which my Passion is to be weighed against the sins of the world! This is the moment to which I looked forward when I first learned my trade at Nazareth, which I decreed at the dawning of creation, when I bade the trees bring forth fruit after their kind. Here is Noah's ark, the refuge of drowning humanity; here is the rod of Aaron, ready to blossom with the flowers of salvation; here is the trunk on which Moses set up the brazen serpent for the healing of my people. Welcome the weight that bows me down, and the roughness that galls my torn flesh, and the shame it bears; for this is my Father's will, this is the token of his Love, this is the stroke of divine justice, cancelling the debt due from a guilty race. Welcome every painful step, the hard road I tread and the stones my feet stumble over; this journey is better than my entry into the Holy City a few days past, more triumphal still, for it is the pageant of self-immolated Love. It was Jacob boasted long ago; he had nothing but a staff with him, when he crossed the Jordan, and now he had come back with two companies behind him. And I, who set out with this Cross of mine now, will return to my Father's kingdom at the head of a great army, all the faithful souls who will love my Cross and carry it in their own lives. This is the sceptre with which I will rule the world; this is the magnet by which, when I am lifted up, I will draw all men unto me.

Now, I am not using the Cross as the type of sorrow or suffering, though it is often so used in common speech. I am using it as the type of that service, that submission to a will not our own, which falls to the lot of all men simply because we live in a world governed by law; and which goes against the grain with us, because we live in a world which is fallen. Just as the Impenitent Thief had to carry his cross, although he did not accept it or identify himself in any way with the justice which laid it upon him, so even a complete libertine, who is determined to get the utmost selfish pleasure out of life, nevertheless has to obey laws, and chafes continually at the limitation which they put upon his actions. He is restricted by human laws, he is restricted by social conventions, he is restricted by the interference of other people's lives with his own. There is no such thing as a life of complete self-pleasing; and those who aim at it are simply condemning themselves to unhappiness; they will be perpetually out of harmony with the order in which they live.

Most of us, in our moral lives, shoulder the cross of duty very much in the spirit of the Penitent Thief, as I tried just now to outline. We accept the moral law as God's will for us; we admire it in the abstract; we applaud holiness and mortification in the lives of others. But when it comes to the point, duty always presents itself to us, doesn't it, as something disagreeable—generally, too, as something negative; there is something we would like to do if only God's Law wasn't there telling us not to do it—we should like, for example, to do an unkind turn to somebody who has annoyed us, and then, just when we have got it all mapped out in our minds, conscience comes in and warns us that the action we propose is wickedly malicious. All right, then, we won't do it after all. But we don't love conscience any the better for it—a drag, an encumbrance, that's what we feel about conscience.

And then, after a time, the pressure seems to grow too strong, and the cord snaps. The temptation we have so often resisted has been eating away our resistance, it seems, all the time; the pitcher has been to the well once too often. And we go to confession and tell God we are sorry; and we *are* sorry; we know that the law against which we have offended is God's will for us, and in breaking it we have set his will at defiance. And then we make good resolutions; we look forward into the future and see there mapped out before us a whole lot of things which we would rather like to do but know we are not to do, because it would be wrong, because it would be sinful; we must keep ourselves more under control, more under lock and key, in future. That's how our good resolutions look to us, isn't it? And, mind you, I am not saying that a life so spent in a continual uphill fight against our own inclinations is not a Christian life, or that it may not be a heroic Christian life. I am only wondering whether our Lord does not mean us to see that there is an alternative—that there is another way of shouldering the cross of duty which is certainly much happier for us, apparently more natural for us, and quite probably much more effective for us? I mean that we should choose, not the way of mere obedience, but the way of love.

The Penitent Thief bears his cross manfully and makes the best of it, but that's all. He would throw it away if he could; he feels it as an incubus, a drag on his steps. But with our Lord it is different; he likes carrying his Cross. And I think quite certainly the reason why the heroic virtues of the saints are so different from the humdrum virtues of the ordinary Christian is that the saints always went by the way of love.

Well, you say, that is for the saints; it has nothing to do with people like me. But I wonder, is that really true? Even as a matter of psychology, isn't it probable that all this negative business has a kick-back which is bad for us? I mean, if you sit down and say to yourself, "I wish I found it easier to like Mrs. Jones! Of course, she's a bore, but she can't help that; and she treated her first husband abominably, but that's all ancient history, and nothing in the world would induce me to bring *that* up, naturally. As for her behaviour to me, well, it really has been shocking; but I expect that prejudices me against her, so I am the last person who can safely sit in judgement on her. Yes, I *will* try to like Mrs. Jones"—if you go through all that process, it's fairly obvious that in your efforts to like Mrs. Jones you have been stamping a very unfriendly picture of her deeper and deeper into your imagination. Your resolution to avoid a sin against charity has re-awakened in you all the old echoes of uncharitable criticism. Where the sixth commandment is concerned, even the moral theologians warn us that we must be careful not to indulge our imaginations when the mention of such sins crops up in our prayer, or in our examination of conscience. But I wonder if it doesn't apply to other commandments too? When you are nursing a grievance, for example, how difficult it is to make any acts of the will about forgiving the injury done to you, without feasting the imagination on all the details of your grievance!

Well, you ask, how would the saint react to the mention of the same Mrs. Jones? I don't know; I wish I did. I suppose it would be something like this: "Mrs. Jones! It's curious how her interests never seem to be the same as mine. In fact, she rather bores me; I suppose I must bore a lot of people in the same way. How odd our judgements of one another are; how limited! Dear God, what does it matter what anybody thinks of me except you? What you think of me, that I am; your thought squares with reality, makes reality what it is. Poor Mrs. Jones, I'm afraid she was a good deal to blame over that first marriage of hers; let's hope she has seen that now and made what amends she could for it. How tragic that we should be able to do so little, afterwards, in the way of making amends! Dear God, what amends can I ever make to *you* for this, and that, and that?

But I'm afraid she's a woman who finds it difficult to get on with people; certainly *I* seem to have got on the wrong side of her somehow, without meaning to. Well, I suppose it all squares out; after all, there are such a lot of people who are far more patient with me than I have ever deserved. And you, dear God, who know exactly the kind of person I am, who are incapable of not noticing it when I wrong you, incapable in a sense of not minding it when I wrong you, you are so much more patient with me than anybody else. Bless Mrs. Jones, and make her patient with me too."

We don't react like that. But I cannot help thinking that is what our Lord is asking us to do.

It seems to me that it is very much easier to understand the Gospels, and a great deal of our Lord's teaching in the Gospels, if we believe that the way of love was meant, not only for a small collection of heroic souls, but for ordinary people like you and me. Above all, if you look at the Sermon on the Mount, and that great fifth chapter of Saint Matthew which is the opening of the Sermon on the Mount, I do not know how you are to find the key to fit it, unless you suppose that our Lord has in mind this contrast between the way of duty and the way of love.

He begins by telling his disciples that unless their justice gives better measure than that of the scribes and Pharisees, they shall not enter into the kingdom of heaven. That sounds strong; that sounds formidable to start with. And then he proceeds to illustrate that by referring to different points of the moral law in detail, catching up the echoes of Mount Sinai and refashioning its code all through. "It was said to the men of old, Thou shalt do no murder; but I tell you that any man who is angry with his brother must answer for it before the court of justice.... It was said, Thou shalt not commit adultery. But I tell you that he who casts his eyes on a woman so as to lust after her has already committed adultery with her in his heart. . . . It was said to the men of old, Thou shalt not perjure thyself; but I tell you that you should not bind yourselves by any oath at all. Let your word be Yes for Yes, and No for No. . . . It was said, An eye for an eye and a tooth for a tooth, but I tell you that you should not offer resistance to injury; if a man strikes thee on thy right cheek turn the other cheek also towards him. . . . It was said, Thou shalt love thy neighbour and hate thy enemy, but I tell you, Love your enemies." The phrases are familiar enough; what are we to make of them?

At first sight it looks, doesn't it, as if the law given from the mount of the Beatitudes differed from the law given from Mount Sinai only in being more stringent, more exacting, in setting up a whole new code of prohibitions, which are to make the path of duty much more complicated and much more arduous for us Christians than it ever was for the Jews under the Old Dispensation. For them, no murder, for us, every outburst of temper is a grievous sin; for them, no adultery, for us, every glance perhaps a necessary matter of confession; for them, no perjury, for us, no formulas of solemn undertaking; for them, no unjust advantage over one who had wronged them, for us, no right even to protest against an injury. Can our Lord really have meant that? Why then does he tell us that his yoke is easy and his burden light when, demonstrably, he is asking more of us than he asked of those who went before?

The answer—you will have guessed it already—is that what our Lord means to contrast here is not so much the content of the two moral laws, his own and that of Moses, as the spirit in which he wants his law to be kept and the spirit in which the law of Moses was kept at that day—the spirit, unfortunately, in which both the law of Moses and the law of the gospel are kept, even now, by all too many of us, inside the Church and out of it. Moses, he says, assumes that the people for whom he is legislating, the children of the Old Covenant, will want to take every advantage they possibly can, will have to be tied down with a series of hard and fast definitions to keep their natural appetites, somehow, in check. But I am legislating for the children of the gospel, and the children of the gospel will not need, ought not to need, this series of prohibitions, because they will not want to do harm; they will love the good for its own sake. They will not need laws telling them not to murder people, because the very emotion of hatred will find no lodging, or no fixed lodging, in their hearts. No need to caution them against adultery, because they will love purity and have no eyes for what is forbidden them. No need to warn them about the solemn nature of an oath, and the wickedness of perjury; if they have said a thing, they will want to be as good as their word; in their simplicity it will not occur to them to do otherwise. No need to forbid unjust retaliation; the very idea of retaliation will be foreign to their outlook; loving me, they will love their fellow-men, my children, and be always wanting to give and to forgive. He needs no dangerposts who walks steadily in the way of love.

Picture to yourself a boat moored in the open sea, the sport of winds and tides. It is moored securely enough; it does not drift away and get lost. But it is continually being forced this way and that, farther and farther, until suddenly the rope tightens and it is pulled up with a jerk, only to cruise off in another direction and get pulled up with a jerk again. That jerk, you know, is not good for it; it is testing the strength of the rope and gradually fretting it away. Let that be our image of a soul which serves God only by the way of duty. All the time it is being drifted this way and that by the tides of its own corrupt nature, by the winds of bad example and bad company. It seems as if it must be swept away into sinful courses—but no, the rope pulls it up at the last moment, the rope of obedience; and so it cruises off until the rope of obedience is needed to pull it up again. Once more, that jerk of the rope is not good for it; the resistance is being gradually fretted away. And now think of the same boat moored in a safe harbour. It is moored, just in case anything should go wrong, but as a matter of fact the moorings are never submitted to any strain; it rides peacefully in the calm waters, never moving this way or that sufficiently to draw the rope taut. Let that be our image of a soul which serves God by the way of love. The commandments are there, the spirit of obedience is there, but it is not called upon to act; the soul is no longer at the mercy of wind or tide, that it should need the warning tug of the rope to keep it in position; it rides securely on that calm surface, the Love of Jesus Christ.

But, you say, most Christians can never hope to attain anywhere near such perfection as that. Well, it is true as a matter of observation that most Christians don't. But then, I'm sorry to say, most Christians seem to be content with the very minimum that is asked of them in the way of worship and of spiritual exercises. Most Christians never read a spiritual book of any sort; most Christians don't go into retreat after they leave school; most Christians are content to rush into the confessional at the last moment and never seriously consult a priest about the state of their souls; most Christians would look at you with surprise if you suggested that it was possible for an ordinary layman to make a meditation; most Christians allow about five minutes for thanksgiving after Communion, instead of kneeling on a little and affording our Lord the opportunity he wants to visit them with his inspirations. There are such a lot of things most Christians don't do. And so they drag on, with the cross of duty laboriously carried on their unwilling shoulders; are they meant to be serving God like that? Are you meant to be serving God like that? Let us ask him, if he will not teach us, instead, the way of love.

XV

DEATH AS ACHIEVEMENT

In the poetry of Homer, one of the earliest literary legacies spared to us from the ruins of antiquity, there is an odd, rare word used to describe the ending of a war. "When he had wound off the skein of war"—that is the phrase used, and you see, at once, its appropriateness. War is the last desperate remedy we invoke when the world's politics have grown so tangled that there is no unravelling the knots by any other means. And whatever horrors, whatever tragedies, it may have involved, the man who has brought a war to a successful conclusion can at least congratulate himself on this—he has wound off the skein of war; there are no loose, ragged ends left now, no puzzling loops; everything is tidied up, the world has become a perfect round again, the task is achieved.

So we tried to tell ourselves, in spite of all appearances, till yesterday. We had seen, in our time, what was perhaps the greatest national deliverance in all our history. And, as we got back our breath, and had time to take stock of what was happening, as we compared the world whose lights went out in 1939 with the world into which light began to filter back, slowly and fitfully, in 1945, what could we claim to have achieved? We had brought hostilities to an end, but we had not wound off the skein of war. Everywhere there were loose ends and ambiguous loops. We had achieved an epic; we had not achieved finality.

Have we any right, indeed, to expect finality, completion, achievement, in human affairs at all? We are so subject to flux and change; so slender are the ties which bind one generation to the next. In art, in literature, one century despises what was prized by the century which went before it; in philosophy, the commonplaces of to-day were the paradoxes of yesterday; even the scientists construct a new world-picture, quite different from any we knew in the past. Everything flows past us; every certitude melts away under our grasp; how should we expect the human race, as it shuffles across the stage of history, ever to reach a definite milestone, turn a definite corner, cross a definite barrier? We are always blundering on—surely that is the true account of it, from one folly to the next, from one tragedy to the next. Let us not flatter ourselves with the idea that we have solved any problems, asserted, beyond contradiction, any principles; let us be content if we have managed to escape from one world-nightmare without plunging into another. That is the mood, I think you can say without exaggeration, of nearly every thinking person to-day.

Is there, then, no finality in human affairs? Must we think of ourselves, not as mountaineers, ever breasting a new slope on our ascent, but as sailors ever mounting the crest of a new wave, only to find a fresh trough to sink into? If we are tempted to feel like that, one utterance ought to give us pause; a single word spoken by a condemned Visionary who broke his heart on a gallows nineteen hundred years ago: "It is achieved." Not "It is finished", not "It is all over", as if he were merely congratulating himself that the kindly opiate of death was putting an end, at last, to his intolerable pain. No; it is achieved; the last stone has been added, to crown the edifice; the last mite has been paid, to extinguish the debt; the last stroke of the brush has swept across the canvas, to eternalize the masterpiece; it is achieved.

It was an extraordinary claim. A few days ago his followers in Jerusalem were going out to meet his followers from Galilee, staging a Messianic coup d'état; where are they now? Of his closest friends, one has committed suicide, one has disowned him, the rest have fled. He told us that if he were lifted up he would draw all men unto him; he has been lifted up for three hours and has made one convert. Ask anyone who knows the ways of the world, and he will tell you what has happened. It is the old story of the idealist who believes that a spiritual movement can make its way in spite of brute force; he is so confident of his own good intentions that it does not seem possible he should fail; God would interfere with the course of history by a miracle, rather than let him fail. And then, he is too successful; authority grows alarmed; brute force reasserts itself, and the spell he cast on men's minds suddenly breaks like tow. It has happened so often; this is but one fresh instance of the ever-recurring human tragedy. Point to it, if you will, as a heroic instance, a supreme instance of the inevitable struggle between right and might; but do not make an epoch of it; do not tell us that it has achieved anything. One more Prophet has learned what welcome it is the world gives to prophets; that is all.

But from that picture of irremediable disaster springs our faith. Faith is a quality which is not merely independent of common human calculations; it is a quality which rejoices to set them at defiance. Faith is like the lever, which must find a fulcrum that pushes in the opposite direction before it can exert its force. Faith is like those rock-plants which languish unless you plant them in barren soil. Faith is like the undertow in the mill-stream, that is attracted where we thought it would be repelled. And it would not, if it could, have chosen any other setting for the supreme event in the world's history than the setting of Good Friday. He who came to earth to share the life of common men welcomed—how could he otherwise?—the common fate of men, wished to die, as other men have died before and since, at the hands of tyranny masquerading as justice; God made Man, should he aspire to earthly crowns? If he said, "It is achieved", it was because he had eyes for something other than the gaping crowd beneath him, and the city walls, and the fading light, and the windswept hill. In the supernatural order, which was the native haunt of his mind, great issues were being fought out, of which this commonplace tragedy was only a shadow, cast on the screen of time. He saw the whole history of the human race meeting in a point, and a door unlocked, and a puzzle solved all in a moment as every piece fitted into its place; he saw the righting of a wrong, the lifting of a ban, the fulfilment of an incalculable purpose.

If we would interpret, so far as lies within the compass of our groping minds, that vision of the Crucified, let us notice this first, that the word he uses is a word his evangelist has used, only two verses before. "Jesus, knowing that all things were now achieved, that the Scripture might be fulfilled, said, I thirst." It is a strange fact that here, as on at least one other occasion, our Lord deliberately acted in such a way as to secure that the Old Testament prophecies might be fulfilled. Have you ever looked down from a hill-side, and identified a hamlet lying at your feet with this or that name on the map, and suddenly caught yourself saying "That's where it *ought* to be"? As if it were the business of the real world to correspond with the map, not the other way round? So, sometimes, the Gospels will talk as if the fulfilment was for the sake of the prophecy, not the prophecy for the sake of its fulfilment. I suppose if we could see eternal truth as it is, that would not surprise us. The prediction of future events, when it comes from God, is as much a part of his scheme as the events themselves. And I think the first meaning of that cry, "It is achieved", is simply this: that our Lord saw in the life he had lived a groove marked out for him by prophecy; he had filled in the blueprint of Messianic expectation to the last detail, never once smudging its outlines. He had lived a decreed life.

No, King David had not been wrong when he sang of his enemies parting his garments among them and casting lots upon his vesture, of being given gall to drink, of having his hands and feet pierced, of being betrayed by his familiar friend, of being accused by false witnesses. Isaiah had not been wrong when he wrote of the Suffering Servant who would be led like a lamb to the slaughter, whose stripes would be the healing of his people. Jeremiah had not been wrong when he poured out, in accents too poignant to be justified by his own experience, the complaints of the rejected Prophet. Noah's ark fell into place, and the brazen serpent in the wilderness, and the paschal lamb, and the sacrifice of Isaac; it all fitted in with Calvary, which meant, more importantly, that Calvary fitted in with it. Type and anti-type clashed like a pair of cymbals, to lend music to that cry of triumph, "It is achieved."

And perhaps our Lord thought not only of the revelations God had made to his favoured prophets, his chosen people. Had there not been, among heathen peoples too, frantic guesses at the truth which now proved not so far from the mark, after all, about the king who must be slain by his people, so that a virtue, an influence, should pass in some strange way from him to them; about the divine hero who died and must be mourned every year, when springtime came round; and so on? I like to think that he who had not left himself without a witness even in the heathen world made something, too, of these distorted follies of ours, like the artist who, with a few bold strokes, gives meaning and coherence to a child's picture.

Perhaps, too, he saw what you and I can never see, what we were telling one another just now that we despaired of ever seeing—the meaning of history. Over his head fluttered an insulting handbill, with the words boldly inscribed on it, "Jesus of Nazareth, the king of the Jews". And they were written, you will remember, in Hebrew, and Greek, and Latin. Hebrew, and Greek, and Latin, the three languages of the ancient world which have produced real literatures; the three separate types of genius which have contributed most to the formation of human thought. At the moment of the Christian era, those three strands had met in one. The world was governed and organized by the imperial greatness of Rome. Its culture, its language, were those of the subtle and speculative Greeks. Under these two influences the known world of our Lord's day had become one, as never before. Wide as that world, mingling with it everywhere yet mysteriously apart from it, were the scattered representatives of God's ancient people, the Jews, with a surer grasp of divine things than Greek or Roman had ever attained. The conquests of Nabuchadonosor, of Alexander, of Pompey had all contributed to make a nest, as it were, in which God's revelation would be cradled. A strange purpose, little dreamt of by the men who, under God's Providence, carried it out.

It was achieved now, the unexpected dénouement to which all the struggles of the Mediterranean world had been leading up. Meanwhile, the future as well as the past lay within our Lord's view; did he not look forward, down the long avenues of history, and see the part which the Christian faith was to play in its development, as something achieved? We are too near it to make out the pattern for ourselves; nay, we are of it, we are making it. To us, the Christian tradition seems, when all is said and done, a faint and precarious influence in the counsels of a world so swayed by greed and love of conquest; it disappears and reappears in the flood, now neglected, now, for a moment, formidable.

We are not conscious of achievement here; but he (let us remind ourselves again) saw things with other eyes; and to him there was pattern where we find only chaos.

But indeed, all our notions of world-history are an illusion. The only history that matters is the history of the individual soul, your soul or mine, working out its eternal salvation. And for every human soul that ever was or will be created, that twilight afternoon on the hillside above Jerusalem was the acid test of its character and its destiny. Satan only fell when he refused to serve a crucified Master; and we must needs believe that, in some mysterious way, each soul which shares Satan's doom has made Satan's choice. Essentially, the achievement of Calvary was the salvation of every soul that ever will be saved. Far as our Lord's eye could reach, further than human eye could reach, the hills that stand round Jerusalem were peopled for him, that day, with all the myriads of souls that will ever struggle into heaven—his children, playing about the foot of the Cross. The Father of the world to come—that is one of his titles; and he looks down with an indulgent eye on all these, his regenerate; only, they must not worry their Mother just now; see, she is in tears.

Their Father, in the sense that every grace by which their souls live comes down from him in the supernatural order, as directly as their natural bodies come down from Adam. But he is comforted, there on the Cross, not only with the joy of parenthood, but with the pride of the successful teacher. His whole life has been a masterpiece of living; and the foot of the Cross is not only the nursery of Christ's children; it is also their school. This is the final touch, which makes the masterpiece complete. Even his most forward scholars, those twelve who have been with him in all the experiences that have tested him—what was it they were saying, only last night, at supper? They were quarrelling about which of them should be the greatest. Let them creep out of their hiding-places now, gather round the Cross, and see if they cannot spell out their lesson. It is written in three languages, so that a world may have access to it: "Jesus of Nazareth, the king of the Jews". And this is his throne; will they still go about asking which of them is to be the greatest? Every moment in the life of Rabbi Jesus of Nazareth was spent in teaching; patiently, day after day, he has hammered in his instructions; and now, on this vivid blackboard, their final instructions are written large; whose fault will it be, if they are not finished scholars now?

It is achieved, not merely in the sense of a work finished, not merely in the sense of a lesson taught, but in the sense of a life saved. Always, in the last resort, we must love the life and death of Jesus of Nazareth not for what they did on our behalf, not for any lesson they teach us, but for what they were in themselves, a perfect offering made to God. That, after all—you have only to read any page of Saint John to be assured of it—was the direct, conscious motive of every act in his career, not to win your salvation or mine, not to inspire us or help us out with our problems, but to do the will of the Father who had sent him. And the last moment of life, for every human creature, is not merely the moment at which it finishes, but the moment at which it achieves. The supreme sacrifice which the creature makes to its Creator is the act of dying—that act by which, in acceptance of his will, it is content to resign its creaturely existence; to become, as it were, a nothing instead of a thing; to be nothing, and let him be everything. "Father, into thy hands I commend my spirit"—that self-annihilation on the part of Incarnate God was *the* achievement of his life. May that, in our measure, be our achievement too; "Father, into thy hands . . ."; this spirit, thy creature; take it and do with it what thou wilt, make of it what thou wilt; it is thine.

XVI

THE ENTOMBMENT

Whenever we try to contemplate the figure of our Lady in the Gospels, she always defeats our purpose; she points us away from herself, points us to her Son. It was her mission and her resolve while he remained on earth, to hide her personality behind his; she would be like the vessels of the altar, which, precious themselves, elude notice because of the far more precious Thing which they contain. Our Lady at Bethlehem will not receive our homage; she is only the ciborium, she tells us, through which the Bread of Life has come to us; look at this Baby, stretching out its feeble hands—this is God. Our Lady on Calvary stands close, but veils herself, as the paten is veiled by the corporal when the Consecration is made; she is only the paten, and our eyes should be for the Host; look at this condemned Malefactor, sighing out his life—this is God. And when he is taken down from the Cross, it is his face, not hers, that catches our attention; her arms are only the monstrance, and our eyes should not be for the monstrance but for what it carries; look at this lifeless corpse which I embrace—this is God.

For our present purpose let us not direct our attention, or our devotion, towards her. Let us join our attention and our devotion with hers as she looks down upon the body of her Divine Son; let us see it with her eyes, and allow ourselves to be penetrated by her sentiments. And then, when we have thought for a little about his death, let us shift the perspective and look forward to our own death. She will be there, please God, to help us when we die, to help us on the other side of death; we are her children too.

Think first of the history of that Body—its remote history. It was formed, by a miraculous conception, in the womb of a Virgin; it was born by birth as miraculous as the miracle by which, on Easter Day, it will rise again from its dark tomb, leaving the stone in its place at the door. It was suckled at the breast of a sinless creature; and although it went through, before and after birth, all the stages of development through which our bodies go, the soul which informed it was personally united to the Godhead. A Body, then, mysterious in its origins, unique in its worth, incalculable in its significance—and yet here it lies like the body of any other son of Adam, quite still, quite powerless.

Then think of its more recent history, which you may read in those cruel scars that disfigure it. Those are the eyes that wept over the ingratitude of Jerusalem, from that brow the sweat started out in Gethsemani; that cheek still blushes, you might think, from the shame of the traitor's kiss. The wrists are still swollen, where they were bound when he was led away; the back is scarred with long weals, the piteous talley of his scourging; the forehead has bled where the thorns pricked it; the shoulders are bruised from the heavy burden they bore; the knees, where they collapsed on the ground outside the city gate. More prominent still, and more unsightly, the torn flesh of hands and feet where the nails went through them, the deep cleft in the side. "No beauty, as we gaze on him, to win our hearts"—in that broken frame we hardly recognize the appearance of a man; and this is God.

Think, now, of what that Body was to him who wore it yesterday—the material complement of a soul completely sanctified; the smile with which he forgave the sinner traced its lines round that mouth; the sighs he uttered over man's unbelief filled those lungs; those brows were contracted with indignation at the senseless pride of the Pharisees. The material source, too, of the mortifications which his soul encountered; it was that body which hungered when he fasted in the wilderness; those are the feet which tired on the roads of Galilee when he went about doing good; those are the eyelids which ached when he denied himself sleep; that is the throat that was parched with thirst by the side of Jacob's well. The material accomplice, even, of his marvellous works—the woman who had an issue of blood did but touch the hem of the garments it wore, and virtue went out of that body to heal her infirmity; this hand touched how many fevered brows, lifted up how many cripples and gave them strength to walk; from those lips went forth the word of healing which lightened so many sorrows, reversed so many tragedies, the word which, only yesterday it seems, pierced through the stone that lay against the tomb of Lazarus, and bade the dead man come forth—now, that voice in its turn is silent with the silence of the tomb; that hand is motionless; that body wants, not only the theandric virtue which once radiated from it, but the power to stir its own muscles.

His Spirit, that he breathed out on the Cross, resigning it into his Father's hands, still pursues the same beneficent course. Translated into a world of disembodied spirits, the spirits of the just who died before Calvary, it has brought to them the light and refreshment they longed for; instead of being imprisoned like other human souls, it has disprisoned the others and summoned them to share its own reward. But the Body that was its partner lies here according to the wont of human bodies; nothing, at least to the outward eye, distinguishes its lot from theirs. Our faith, we thought, had been taxed enough, recognizing the eternal Godhead under the form of a little child on his mother's breast, or a poor labouring man in a Galilean workshop, or a prisoner condemned by legal sentence and hung on a Cross to die. But see, here is one more demand faith makes of us; we have to recognize eternal God under the form of a dead body, ripe for the tomb.

For remember, this is God—is, not was; we are not to speak as if the separation of soul from body in our Lord's human nature meant that half of that nature, its material part, ceased even for a moment to be the vehicle of the divinity with which the Incarnation had wedded it. The Hypostatic Union is not something which links the Godhead to the rest of our Lord's humanity through the medium of his soul; it is a complete union between God and man, which does not cease even when soul is separated from the body; God laid in the sepulchre is God still. Soul and body are integral parts of a single whole; and in the Incarnate every part of that whole was, and remains, divine.

Thou wilt not suffer thy Holy One, said King David, to see corruption; in our Lord's sepulchre the victory of our nature over death was manifested and achieved. The preservation of his sacred body from that law by which our bodies return to the dust whence they came, and are commingled with it, was the earnest of our own resurrection at the last day. Matter is not, after all, something in itself ignoble, something that clogs and imprisons us; it, too, is part of us and will one day be part of us again, though now glorified and etherialized in such a measure that our minds cannot conceive it. Both spirit and body in man must, at last, triumph over death, since spirit and body are both divinized in the Incarnation.

When you see some familiar representation of the Pietà, it is natural to think of our Lady, in the first instance, as making a kind of sacerdotal gesture; she is offering the consummated sacrifice to Almighty God. Her eyes are lifted upwards, not as if protesting against a crime, but as if pleading an immolation. Do you remember how Joseph's brethren, after they had sold him to the Madianites, brought his coat back home with them, the coat of many colours, and showed it to Jacob to make him believe that his son was dead? "Know now", they said to him, "whether this be thy son's coat or not." So, with outspread arms, our Blessed Lady holds up the dead body of the Crucified, the garment of his humiliation, offers it to the scrutiny of her Maker; "Know now whether this be thy Son's body, or not." And he, looking upon it, recognizes in that generous profusion of life-blood the seal of a charity which cannot be less than divine; recognizes in that visage, marred beyond the sons of men, the unmistakeable character of the Son of God.

But at the same time, she is showing the burden she carries in her arms to us. If she is at the altar, she is also in the pulpit. We are to see, there in her arms, the perfect model, the perfect masterpiece, of human dying. We are to see what death means for us; how her Son's death has transformed it for us, is to be the inspiration of ours, was, in a sense, the anticipation of ours. And first, it is a real body that she shows us—not some phantasmal appearance, flesh and blood like ours. It is not something negligible, then, this body of ours; it is a true part of us; it demands our care, deserves our reverence; separation from it is something as it were unnatural—death is not merely slipping off a garment that is outworn.

Yes, a body like ours, but not doomed, as ours are, to see corruption. And yet, how did our Lord treat his body? You would think, to watch the way we Christians order our lives, that it was the other way about. We are so concerned with cosseting the body and pampering it, spend so much care, even, on the outward appearance of it, give in so easily to its complaints if it is tired out or indisposed—this body which is corruptible and is passing on its way into corruption, itself and all its activities native to a world of dust. Our Lord hungered and thirsted, watched and laboured, had nowhere to lay his head; he didn't spare that body of his, that was to rest but two days in the sepulchre; and how do we treat ours, that will part company with us from the hour of death till the general Resurrection?

Our bodies will lie motionless, one day, in the arms (please God) of the Church, that kindly mother who has a place and a plan for everything. Meanwhile, what of our souls? What is more terrifying than the thought of a soul, one's own, a naked soul, ushered, all unacclimatized, into the airs of eternity? We are daunted by what seems the complete discontinuity of the experience. And yet, there cannot be absolute discontinuity; that moment after death will have some relation to the moment which went before. We must look, then, at the last moment of our Lord's life, so that it may be a model for the last moment of ours. "Father," he says, "into thy hands I commend my spirit." The metaphor of the verb is that of the man who puts his money into a bank. The man who puts his money into a bank makes, to that extent, an act of confidence in the bank's solvency and honesty; so that the phrase which our Lord uses at the moment of death, for our example, will be an act of confidence in God, his omnipotence, his infinite goodness. When a man is told, on his death-bed, to resign himself to the death God wills for him, that does not mean shrugging his shoulders and saying, "Well, there is no getting out of this, so I may as well make up my mind to go through with it." To resign yourself at the hour of death is to make a supreme act of confidence in God; to protest your conviction that the form of death he wills for you, the moment of death he wills for you, is the best form, is the best moment; you are going to leave everything absolutely to him; you are prepared to let your spirit *go* into his hands—relax all effort, and let him do everything. In so far as you have resigned yourself to death, your soul will find itself, after death, securely in his hands; it will be the expected that happens to it. But that act of resignation will not be easy to make on your death-bed—if you have a death-bed—unless you have some practice in it beforehand. Perhaps sometimes—perhaps when we are making a retreat?—it would be a good thing to rehearse beforehand that act of resignation.

Our Lord was judged by men and condemned to death. His enemies, as if to declare the irrevocability of the sentence, put a stone over the door of his tomb and sealed it; nothing more could happen now. But man's judgements are not irrevocable; and the very parade of legal precision which the chief priests adopted did but serve to vindicate the truth of his Resurrection. When God judges man, *his* judgements *are* irrevocable; and we know that immediately after death your soul and mine will be judged and their destiny will be sealed, irrevocably, for all eternity. They will be as powerless, then, to merit or to affect their own destiny as our dead bodies will be powerless to move in their coffins. In that most solemn moment of all our existence, that moment for which we were created, our judgement, what shall we be thinking about? Our sins? Our confessions, whether they were entire? Our contrition, whether it was genuine? The opportunities we had of doing something for God, and let them slip? The graces we wasted through our infidelity? And on the other side, the little we did do for God, the graces we corresponded with, and made something of them?

Perhaps. Indeed, if the sentence is to go against us, and we are to be exiled for all eternity from the presence of

God, it is natural to suppose that such thoughts will occupy our mind to the exclusion, for the moment, of everything else. What we did, and what we might have done—how little more of effort, of courage, of independence it would have needed to make us do the right thing instead of the wrong thing, take the right turning instead of the wrong turning, here and here and here. Yes, if the sentence is to go against us, if we are to be lost. But let us not consider that possibility, just now. If we are to be amongst the elect, shall we really be thinking, in that moment when judgement is passed on us, of what we did or did not do, of what we might or might not have done? Surely not. Surely what will be before our eyes will be a body newly taken down from a Cross, a body wounded for our sins, bruised for our iniquities. We shall look upon him whom we have pierced, for it will be he, none other, who judges us; and we shall see, in that moment, not how we betrayed, how we denied, how we crucified him, but how his death saved us, how his scars healed us, how from that pierced side the fountains of sacramental grace flowed, absolution to justify us, Holy Communion to sanctify us. And that Face, which we have so often seen in our imagination looking at us, as it looked at Peter, in reproval of our sins, will show gentle and merry to us, and we shall know that nothing henceforth can ever separate us from him.

And in heaven? "Show unto us the blessed fruit of thy womb, Jesus"—is that only a rhetorical expression? Do we only ask our Lady to win us such grace in this life that we may see our Lord in the next? It may be so. But it seems difficult to believe that we shall have no sight, in heaven, of what Bethlehem was; and if of Bethlehem, why not of Calvary? I like to think, at least, that the three chaplets of the rosary will not show any longer, in heaven, as three separate strands of experience, but somehow as a single tapestry. That seeing them both in their glory, we shall only have to bend sideways, as it were, to catch sight of the eternal truth in a different light—to see a Child resting in his Mother's arms, to see, though it were only for one moment of eternity, our Lord's wounds still bleeding, and our Lady's tears.

HOLY HOUR—THE MASS AND THE LIFE OF CHRIST

i

Our Lord's earthly life divides itself naturally into four periods, differing very much in length, sharply marked off one from another by the changed conditions under which they were lived: first, his birth and the thirty years of obscurity; then the three years or a little less of his public ministry; then the week or, if you will, the three hours of his Passion; then the forty days of his Risen Life before the Ascension. I don't think it is altogether fanciful to see the same fourfold division in that effectual drama which perpetuates his Eucharistic life, the holy Mass. Leaving out those parts of it which are variable, you can see in the priest's attitude during the early part of the Mass a mirror of the humiliation, the self-annihilation, which belongs to our Lord's Infancy; in his attitude at the offertory, a mirror of the self-oblation which was our Lord's public life; in his attitude during the canon, a mirror of the self-sacrifice which inspired our Lord's Passion; in his attitude during the Communion, perhaps less clearly recognizable, a mirror of the glory which shines out from our Lord's Risen Body, and from its acts.

I want to quote what I wrote in a very different connexion once about High Mass at the London Oratory. "The three ministers, dwarfed by the height of the building, seem like ants crawling about in the presence of something immeasurably greater than themselves; the Kyrie and the Miserere nobis of the Gloria sound like what they are, tributes of abject servility to a King whose audience no unclean thing may approach; the spaciousness of the whole setting, music and building and ceremonies, stands for a poor sacrament of that infinitude towards which all this self-annihilating homage is directed." The more you consider the opening part of the Mass, Preparation, Kyrie, and Gloria, the more impressed you will be, I think, with the air of intense diffidence which characterizes the attitude of the priest throughout; see how he has to wait and say a prayer for himself, before he can persuade himself to profane, with unworthy lips, the words of the very Gospel.

And all that is the mirror of the self-abasement by which, and in which, the Word of God became man—not that he humbled himself as being unworthy; but he humbled himself *as if he were* unworthy, to carry out his redemptive task, a refinement of self-humiliation. Just as the priest will not trust himself to enter upon the ceremonies of the great sacrifice till he has grovelled before the throne of God, so in his courtesy our Lord would not be content, in coming to redeem us, with the self-emptying already required of him in becoming man; he would become a child, a baby, speechless, helpless, having to have everything done for him, then to become a working man, quite unknown, quite unimportant, emptying himself utterly as man of the divine dignity which in truth could never leave him. It was the Judica me, the Confiteor, the Kyrie eleison, before the great Mass of his earthly Life. He wanted us to see, surely, that that must be the first stage of our approach to God—self-abasement, getting the position clear to ourselves about what God is and what we are, as a man using a telescope must get his instrument focussed before he begins to take his observations.

The easiest way in which we can make use of our Lord's life and example in our own prayer—much easier, I think, than trying to represent scenes before our eyes and then examining them with the intellect, and then making them the subject for acts of the affections and of the will—is this: as he gives us light, to enter into the dispositions with which he, Incarnate as man, presented himself before his Father, to make them our own, and let our aspirations go out to him in union with them. So, as we start on this hour of prayer before the Blessed Sacrament, let us remember how he began his Incarnate life by humiliating himself; let us remember how he, in the person of his priest, begins the holy Mass by prostrating himself at the foot of the altar; and let our first attitude be one of utter self-abasement. God is our All, and we are his nothing; it is the distance between that all and that nothing that should first occupy our thoughts, bowing us down and crumpling us up with the poignancy of the contrast; we must go to him and ask him to empty us, empty us of self and of self-seeking and of self-regard, his creatures: My God and my all; I am nothing.

ii

The offertory is the part of the Mass which we notice least, unless we happen to be on the altar; we sit down, and take a bit of a rest, and perhaps unconsciously give leave to our attention to wander a bit because there is always the Sanctus bell to wake us up again. That is all wrong, because in a sense it is the part of the Mass in which the congregation really come in, really take a major part in the drama; for the bread and wine are in theory their gifts, being offered by the priest in their name; you are the boy giving your five loaves to Christ through his apostle. It is our offering, a ludicrously unimportant offering of something we can easily afford, our superfluity, nevertheless a kind of token payment, to remind us and to own in the sight of God that he can claim everything, that all we have comes from him. It is oblation without sacrifice; if we use sacrificial language in connexion with it, referring to the bread on the paten as an immaculate host, that is because the shadow of the amazing thing it is to become already hangs over it in our imaginations; it is already earmarked for God, soon to be transformed into something else.

I said we would treat this lesser, unsacrificial offering of the unconsecrated host as the mirror of the self-oblation which was our Lord's public life. The attitude of the priest as he stands holding the paten in front of him, as if saying, "Here it is, heavenly Father, this little thing which we are giving you, take it from me"—that is the attitude in which our Lord is seen all through the account of his life which we read in the Gospels. It is made especially noticeable in Saint John: "Father, glorify thy name"—the man born blind was born blind precisely that he might be cured by a miracle, that the works of God might be made manifest in him, and Lazarus falls sick, not unto death, but for the glory of God—in all his wonderful actions our Lord is pointing away from himself to God as the author of life and light and health. And so with the privations of his life; he goes without food because his meat is to do the will of his Father. All the actions of his life, all the determinations of will which are left to man's choice are, in his Incarnate life, offered, held out to God as a human offering—only of course the dignity of his Divine Person gives them a value in advance of that which naturally belongs to them; his humanity compared to that is only the single drop of water with which the priest mixes the chalice. Because of the Hypostatic Union, any single prayer he uttered, any sigh he breathed, would have been sufficient to redeem the world. But, viewed in itself, this continual offering of all the circumstances of his life was the offering we can all make, we ought all to make, if our lives are to have any supernatural meaning or fruit at all. So far, our Lord's life is one of offering, not strictly of sacrifice; the shadow of the Cross hangs over it all, but the sacrifice has not yet begun. He offers his life to God in the sense of offering all that he does and has; he does not as yet explicitly offer his life in the sense of himself, of all that he is.

Let this, then, be the next attitude of our prayer—to identify our dispositions with the dispositions of our Lord all through his public life, a continual offering of all he had and all he did; let us make the bodily posture of the priest as he stands holding out the paten in front of him a diagram of the soul-posture in which we want to be found, consecrating to God every possession we have, every moment we live, every action, even the seemingly indifferent. The mortification which Lent has for its exterior sacrament is, first and foremost, a reminder and a confession that everything we have comes from God; if it is only giving up sugar in your tea or getting up five minutes earlier in the morning, that is an acknowledgement that sleep and food are gifts which come from him, belong to him, so that he has the right to withhold them from us altogether if he would; once again it is only a token payment we make, when we relinquish a little of what we enjoy to him who could claim all. Our first cry to God was, I am nothing; now we go on from that to, I have nothing. All we have and enjoy comes from him, belongs to him; let us tell him, now, that we hold it only at his disposal, want to refer to him the credit of anything we do, consecrate to him all our pleasures, offer to him all our defeats and discomforts; I have nothing, my God, it is all yours; take it, see, I hold it out before me, giving it back to you.

iii

The attitude of the priest during the canon of the Mass is more obviously and more notoriously symbolical than anything we have been speaking of hitherto. From the moment when the phrase *Benedictus qui venit in nomine Domini* recalls to us the shouts of Palm Sunday to the moment when the particle of the Host falls into the chalice at the Fraction, in memory of our Lord's broken body being committed to the tomb, the action of the Mass is Calvary, reinterpreted in gesture and in atmosphere. Consider the attitude of the priest; he is crucified now, fixed in a posture. He does not turn round, as before, and take us into his confidence with Dominus vobiscum; his back is resolutely turned to us; his attention has left the worshippers, to be concentrated on the Victim. His hands are stretched out, practically the whole time; although nowadays custom allows him to raise the hands without raising the arms much, I suppose that originally he stood in the very attitude of crucifixion, the arms going out at right angles to the body. This world-embracing attitude of the crucified, drawing all men to him, is only interrupted when he is actually using his hands for some specific purpose, and in those two short intervals when he is allowed to think especially of his own friends, of his own patrons, living or dead. From the Consecration onwards, his thumbs and forefingers are pressed together, as if contact with the Host had driven a nail through them. And then there is the long silence, punctuated by sudden liftings of the voice at rare intervals; that must have been the impression which the onlookers felt most vividly about the first great Mass that was celebrated on Calvary. And if the priest is now mystically identified with the victim-Christ, the Host and the chalice are so identified not mystically only but substantially; they are Christ. And Christ in the Host, in the chalice, suffers himself to be handled, to be utilized, to be lifted up and offered and broken. The Passion, as far as that is possible, happens again.

Why did our Lord suffer and die? As we have already reminded ourselves, it was not strictly necessary to our salvation; any gesture of the Incarnate in honour of his eternal Father would have had the satisfactory value needed to procure a world's salvation. He would suffer, he would die, so as to attest Love in the only terms into which, at least in this world of probation, Love can be translated, terms of immolation. When God refused Cain's sacrifice of the fruits of the earth, accepted Abel's sacrifice of a slain victim, he foreshadowed the outpouring of his love that was to be. All the long months of our Lord's ministry, the footsore wanderings, the hunger, the want of sleep, the incessant giving himself out to people who thronged round him and wanted him to do things for them—all that was only preliminary, was only the offering of his time, his health, his strength, not the offering of his life properly so called. It was related to that final gift he made in his Passion as the offertory in the Mass is related to the Consecration in the Mass; it was only a preparation. To show how much he loved us, he wanted to be destroyed for us, consumed for us; he who, as God, was immortal and impassible wanted, as man, to be annihilated as far as it is possible for man to be annihilated. As God, existence is his primary attribute—"I am who am". As man, he would encounter, to the best of man's capacity, non-existence; he would undergo death.

If then we would follow the course I have already laid down for this hour of devotion, we must go beyond the last stage we reached, in which we were offering to God all we did and all we had; we must go further and offer to God all we *are*—annihilate ourselves afresh by putting utterly at his disposal all that will become of us, all that he will make of us, in life and in death; we must abandon ourselves to him, willing all that he wills for us, willing nothing except what he wills for us, and willing that only because he wills it for us. I do not mean that we can effectively turn our backs, in the space of ten minutes or even for the space of ten minutes, on all there is in us of self-love and self-choosing, all the ambitions we foster and all the preferences we feel. We can only abandon ourselves to him in aspiration, adopting that as our deliberate attitude and wishing that it were, praying that it may be more of a reality than it is. We can abandon, not self-love itself, but only the love of self-love. Still, even that is a start on the way of interior mortification. My God, I offer you myself, that nothing which I am; annihilate it as you will, by disappointment, by suffering, by death; I claim nothing as my own, and if I could, I would offer it as my gift to you.

iv

After the Fraction and the commixture, a fresh change comes over the attitude of the priest—I do not mean over his external gestures, but over the character of that prayer, mostly inaudible to the congregation, in which he speaks to God. From the moment at which, in the Consecration, our Lord becomes sacramentally present on the altar, you might expect, mightn't you, that the priest would be talking *to* the sacred Host and the sacred chalice all the time; that he would no longer lift up his eyes to heaven, for where is heaven, if not in the consecrated Species that lie before him? That he would no longer address his prayers to the First Person of the Blessed Trinity, who is present indeed but in no special manner, no more than at other times and in other places, but rather to the Second Person of the Blessed Trinity, who, as Incarnate, is present in a very special manner here and now. Not at all; in the second part of the canon as in the first, the priest goes on addressing himself to God the Father, neglecting, you would say, the Presence of our Lord in the consecrated Species, or using it only as an instrument, as a means and a claim for securing audience. But the moment after the Fraction and the commixture have taken place, this reserve on the part of the priest, if I may so call it, breaks down. The sacramental proximity of his Master is too much for him; he calls thrice on the Lamb of God, present as it had been slain in front of him; pleads, in three separate prayers, with God made Man, for his own needs and for the needs of the Church. He no longer stands erect, turning his eyes to heaven; he crouches down as if to get as near as possible to the God who comes so near to him. And he is no longer offering; he is asking; he must garner to the full the influence of that Presence which his own anointed hands have procured.

The emphasis, you see, has shifted; we no longer think of our Lord under the Sacred Species as the Victim that hangs for us, bound and silent, on Calvary, as that Lamb that is dumb and does not open his mouth. We think of him as Christ Risen, the Lamb as we read of him in the Apocalypse, worthy to unseal the Book of Life, slain once but now revived and revivifying, radiating life, making all things new. Now, how are we to think of our Lord's disposition during his Risen Life? We have considered those early years, when his disposition was one of self-abasement; we have considered the public ministry, when his disposition was that of oblation, making a continual offering of all he did, all he had, consecrating every moment to God; we have considered his Passion and what that meant, the extinction of human existence as far as human existence can be extinguished, in him who as God is Existence itself; what are we to make of those forty days when he still remained on earth, but lived a life which seems so mysterious to us, of which our records are so scanty?

I suppose the simplest thing to say is, that he was living on earth the life which is lived by the blessed in heaven. Of course, so far as the inner fastness of his soul is concerned, that was true all through his earthly life; he enjoyed, without interruption, somehow, the vision of God. But, as risen, even his bodily existence was that of the saints in heaven, so far as that is compatible—there we cannot hope to understand much—with the fact of remaining on earth, in touch with earthly surroundings. And the interior disposition of the soul which corresponds to such an earthly-heavenly existence is one of continual peaceful communion with God, of complete superiority to, immunity from, the distractions and the encumbrances of mortal existence. "When morning came, there was Jesus standing on the shore", so we read about one of his meetings with his apostles, and the Fathers of the Church contrast that peaceful figure standing there on the solid ground with the figure we saw earlier in the Gospel, of the tired, persecuted Son of man who had nowhere to lay his head, and must needs take rest as best he could in the stern of a storm-tossed ship.

This condition of intimate communion with God, and consequently of relative immunity from, detachment from, indifference to, the circumstances of mortality, is one which the saints have attained in their degree. It is attained in a lesser degree even by inferior souls that have tried to abandon themselves to God, and been rewarded by some gift of union, such as we can only guess at, in this life. We cannot attempt to attain such a union, obviously; cannot deserve it, cannot even effectively dispose ourselves for it. But we can aspire to it; we can round off this hour of prayer by putting ourselves in God's hands, and longing for that gift, though we be unworthy of it, and confessing that if we could attain even to the fringe of such interior happiness, it would be worth the sacrifice of all we have and all we are. Come, Lord, take possession of my heart, as thou wilt, in the measure thou wilt, when thou wilt; there shall be no more of striving against the drawing of thy grace, no more holding back through love of creatures to stand in the way of closer union with thee.

XVII

THE SECOND CONVERSION

Only Saint Luke tells us that our Lord turned and looked at Saint Peter on the occasion of his third denial. That denial was, according to Père Garrigou-Lagrange, the occasion of his second conversion. The first was when he was called to leave his nets and follow; that made a Christian of him. The third was the day of Pentecost; that made a saint of him. Between these two, something happened; what is it, this intervening stage which spiritual writers call "the second conversion"?

It is not Saint Peter who turns; it is our Lord who turns. Let us acknowledge that first, both to preserve humility and to arm us against despair; the second conversion is not something we do; it is something God elicits in us; we wait upon a divine initiative. Yet the divine initiative demands a human response. What happened in the council chamber was that our Lord, as we say, "caught Saint Peter's eye". Or was it that Saint Peter caught our Lord's eye? There is a mysterious conspiracy of two wills, when you catch somebody's eye; it is a fitting symbol of the whole mystery of grace.

Let us clear away, at once, some misleading notions. The old-fashioned Protestant idea of conversion differed, or was apt to differ, from ours in three particulars. It was supposed to be a sudden event, which knocked you over like a blow from a sledge-hammer. Now, there is no reason why Almighty God should not deal with souls thus, and no doubt sometimes he does; but a gradual weaning away of the soul from worldliness to God is equally, as far as we know, in accordance with his methods. Again, it was supposed to be something of which you were directly conscious; John Wesley, for example, could tell you exactly when it was that his conversion took place, and what his feelings were—what an interior conviction flooded over him that at last the Love of Christ had come into his heart. Well, so could Pascal; but we Catholics do well to remember that the operations of divine grace in the soul do not necessarily leave any ripple on the surface of consciousness. It may be possible to thank God for a real change of heart which you cannot date within two or three months, or even longer. And besides this, some of the old-fashioned Protestants believed that the grace of conversion, once bestowed, could not be lost: then and there, you were sealed for heaven. Catholic theology knows nothing of a grace which, in theory at least, cannot be forfeited. What we call the grace of perseverance is in reality a series of graces, which must be crowned by a good death before it ensures the hope of a blessed eternity. No, if we are to map out the grace of second conversion in our own lives we shall need a closer scrutiny, and a subtler analysis.

Conversion means a turning—in what direction? The question can be variously answered. Our Lord speaks of being converted and becoming like little children. A turning backwards, towards our origins, towards the innocence of childhood. Again, there are souls so myopically concentrated on the schemes they have in view, the objects they have set before themselves, that they have to be turned inwards, like the young man to whom Saint Philip Neri kept on saying, "Yes, and then?" Others are so beset with scruples and diffidences, so given to self-introspection, that they need to be turned outwards; they want to see God's will, not their own salvation, as the first thing that matters, before they can learn to move easily in the spiritual life.

But I want to think of conversion as a simpler thing than that, a turning away from something, and a turning away to something—a turning away from the love of our sins, a turning away towards the realities of the supernatural life.

The phrase "love of our sins" is not a technical phrase; I only use it because I think we ought to keep the truth rather brutally before our minds. In itself it's inaccurate; we don't exactly love our sins, do we? The man who steals twenty pounds doesn't love the theft; he loves the twenty pounds. It would make no difference to his affection for the sum if he had made it on the race-course. It's the objects with which our sins are concerned that we love—sometimes not even that. When you have lost your temper or have been unkind to somebody, what can you find attractive in that afterwards? What pleasure is it possible to derive from having been drunk? Now we come to think of it, what is the sense of using such an inaccurate expression at all?

I know. But, you see, the Church encourages us to detest our sins. We tell God that we detest our sins when we make an act of contrition; and if we want to gain a plenary indulgence, it is actually part of the conditions attached to it that we should detest our sins. Most of us have wondered before now, on such occasions, whether we really do. We have made, we feel, a rhetorical gesture; we have been through a kind of legal ceremony; but is our attitude towards our sins really altered? Do we really detest them? And yet, why not? What is the difficulty about detesting them, if they are as boring as we said just now? Think of some inglorious sin which lies in the remote past, some lie you told at school. In all honesty, can you say that there is any part of your nature, however corrupt, which derives satisfaction now from the circumstance that that lie was told? When we say that we detest our sins, do we only mean that we detest the memory of those self-indulgences which gave pleasure to sense at the time, a memory cherished now, by our lower natures, only in the hope that they might be repeated?

I don't think that can be all. We are too ready, as a rule, to forget that Almighty God gave ten commandments on Mount Sinai, not just two. There must be something in the general sinfulness of our own natures which we are prone to love, and which the Church, therefore, bids us disavow. Should we put it in this way—that each of us has a picture of himself, sins and all, which he loves with a kind of Narcissus-love, though in his calmer and more recollected moments he does not approve of it? I don't think even that will do. So many of our sins are weaknesses, blots, belittlements of our own stature, that we can hardly approve of ourselves in cold blood for being what we are. The scandalmonger, for example, is he really glad, afterwards, that he told that malicious story? The idle man, does he really look forward to the prospect of a wasted day? Even from a quite human, quite natural point of view, any one of us can find defects in himself which he would sooner be without, and some of these are sins. He would improve, if he could, that image which is conjured up in his mind when he thinks about himself. What need, then, that he should be told to detest that image? If he is a man of common human modesty, he detests it already.

No, I think we want to dig deeper. I may be utterly wrong about this, and I dare say the theologians will haul me over the coals for it. But I think the thing we love, the thing we ought to detest, is something of which we are only partly conscious, and our love for it is a partly conscious love. It is not an image which we set before our minds; it is an idol at the back of our minds, hidden away and swathed round with rags of pretence. And it is in the dark recesses of our minds that we go on worshipping it.

Our nature, our corrupt nature, the thing which hits out when we are annoyed, reaches out when some allurement is offered to the senses, draws itself up to its full height when it is insulted in any way—the hidden self which comes out when a man is drunk, for example, or when some acute situation has made him lose control of himself. It is that hidden nature which is there all the time, only we forget that it is there, and which we love; only we forget that we are loving it.

I think that is what Saint James means in that rather mysterious passage we all know so well about the man who is a hearer of the word and not a doer. He is like a man who looks at his natural face in a glass and straightway forgets what manner of man he was. That doesn't mean that he forgets what the law was, what the law said. No, it means surely that in that glimpse of the law he saw himself, his inner nature, as it really was, but it was only for a moment—he went away and forgot the corruption he had seen in his own soul, just as those of us who are not favoured with good looks can shave in the morning and then go downstairs forgetting what ugly brutes we looked. I think that is what Saint Paul means in that curiously frank chapter he gives you in the epistle to the Romans about having the will to do something, and doing just the opposite. "My action does not come from me", he says; "it comes from the sinful principle that dwells in me"; this hidden nature of ours, bottled up and swathed away underground, suddenly peeps out at us like a ghost, and we have sinned.

It doesn't need to be said that we shall not, in this life, rid ourselves wholly of this handicap of corrupt nature which descends to us from the Fall. And I don't even mean that most of us will attain any touch of real sanctity; with the saints, this principle of corrupt nature seems present indeed, but neutralized, like a poison in the system that is held in check by inoculation. No, I only mean that there surely is a dividing line somewhere in the lives of Christian people, which you can call the second conversion. People who have not yet crossed that line may be fighting against their temptations and overcoming them, sometimes with heroic resistance, and, please God, will attain heaven in great numbers, but they still hanker after this corrupt principle of nature which is at the roots of their being. Whereas those who have crossed the line have achieved a kind of poise, a kind of equilibrium, that is quite different; they still have temptations and sometimes yield to them; they still have sinful tendencies, but they have fallen out of love with their sins. Corrupt nature is no longer their romance.

I have been going on too long talking about what is, after all, only the negative side of the question, telling you what it is we turn away from when the second conversion is achieved in us. What is really much more important, because more positive, is what we turn towards. Only this part of my subject creates, I think, still more difficulties of definition. Let me approach it in this way; am I wrong in thinking that what retards spiritual progress in many of us is a fear of the supernatural? Once more I am speaking of a motive which is only half-consciously present to our minds; if it peeps out, we smother it with pious ejaculations. But aren't we, many of us, all too much like children that have just learned to swim and haven't yet the courage to go out of their depth? So that they give a few kicks, and the sixth or seventh touches the ground, and they bob up terribly pleased with themselves for having swum six strokes? I feel there are a lot of us Christian people to whom the supernatural world, in which we conscientiously believe, is nevertheless a foreign element, which somehow frightens us—especially when we read the lives of the saints, and the record of their bleak, uncomfortable goings-on. We are really afraid at the back of our minds, if we would be honest with ourselves, that this religion of ours is a dangerous kind of business, and if we aren't careful it will sweep us off our feet. We shall find ourselves wanting to do the sort of thing the saints did. No man can see God, was the old Jewish principle, and not die. And we, in something the same way, have a kind of superstitious fear that if we went one step too far in the following of the saints, we might lose our balance and topple over, and heaven knows where it would end.

That is a kind of fear which, if we have any generosity of nature, our conscious reflexions will fight down. But it is succeeded by a different kind of fear, at once more complicated and more reputable. The saints, we think to ourselves, or half-think to ourselves, were people who found a tremendous alternative facing them; they could see God wanted them to do something which would cost them a great deal, and the choice was left to them whether they would fall in with God's scheme or not. But now, what if the same alternative were offered to me, and I made (do I not know myself?) the wrong choice? If I were like the rich young man, who turned away sorrowful, because he had great possessions? And we still fear God's invitation to mount higher, not (consciously at least) because we don't want to go higher, but because we are afraid, if the invitation came, we wouldn't accept it. We go into retreat, and the fear is always at our elbow. We go out of retreat, almost saying to ourselves, "Thank God, nothing's happened *that* time."

Well, you know, there I think we are rather like horses shying at something which is much too small, by rights, to be able to frighten them. They say, don't they, that horses see things twice their size, and that is why they so easily fall into an unaccountable panic. And I think, if we are afraid of sanctity, it is partly because we forget how very gently and gradually God leads souls on; how many levels of the Christian life there are, and how comfortably close to the ground we shall still be if he invites us to go up one! No, we're really just in the same position as the children who won't go out of their depth. Swimming only begins to become fun when you have committed yourself to the new element. And the Christian life only begins to take on its proper outlines, to function in its real medium, if we consent to become the castaways of divine grace. The supernatural world is for us, by right of baptism, our proper element; in it we shall find ourselves. It is because we cling to this strange amphibious instinct in our natures that religion remains the laborious thing it is to most of us, the unnatural thing it seems to most of us. We are trying to make the best of two worlds, and sacrificing both.

Saint Peter's denial, we may believe, was the occasion of his second conversion. The one thing his generous nature clearly had to learn was self-distrust. To some of us, less generous by nature, the lesson, considered merely as a lesson, comes more easily. Distrust ourselves? When did we ever do anything else? We are unequal, no one could be more conscious of it than we are, to so high a vocation as the vocation Christ offers us. But, to proceed from that distrust of self to trust in God—that is a different matter. Trust in God is not a mere reasoned calculation, such as any Christian may easily make for himself, that we are all in God's hands all the time and as we have to depend on him for so much it is only reasonable to recognize that we depend on him altogether. Trust is an overbalancing of our whole weight, into his arms. We have the choice between doing it now, or on our death-beds.

I say, we have the choice; but I have been betrayed into the very mistake we are trying to avoid. No, let us remind ourselves again that when we talk of a second conversion we are talking, not of something we want to do for our Lord, but of something we want our Lord to do in us. Let us ask him to effect this alteration in our lives, gradually, if he will, imperceptibly, if he will, leaving us, if he will, a prey to all the old scruples, all the old despairs—but just that touch of his artistry which will turn our cold blueprint into a masterpiece!

XVIII

THE USE OF GOD'S CREATURES

I want to talk now about our use of creatures, that is to say, about the theory and practice of mortification in the Christian life—I mean voluntary mortification—not that we should talk lightly of *in*voluntary mortifications. They are the best of all; God arranges them, not we, and therefore we can be quite certain that they are good for us, if we will meet them in the right way. They are the best of all; the fact that we can't get out of them, that we are only making a virtue of necessity, means that they can't be a serious temptation to spiritual pride. But I want to talk now about our *voluntary* mortifications.

There is one special reason for wanting to tackle the subject just now; it seems to me there is, at the moment, a certain hesitation in Catholic thought on the subject. There is, at the moment, a certain reaction among Catholics, I will not say against asceticism, but against the way in which asceticism has been preached. There are, we are told, two ways of using creatures as a means of getting nearer to God. One is the way of negation, denying yourself things which you enjoy so as to be able to "offer them up" to God, rooting out the love of creatures, like weeds, so as to leave room for the Love of God to grow more freely in us. The other is the way of affirmation, accepting all that God gives us and using our gratitude for innocent pleasures, our admiration of all the beauty around us, to raise our souls up to God. Of course, this way has its perils; we have to be on our guard against selfishness; we have to make sure that this or that enjoyment does not bring with it the occasions of sin. But, as long as we are on our guard against such perils, this way of affirmation (we are told) is at least as good as the other—perhaps in a way better than the other, because after all isn't it rather inconsistent to say thank-you to God for his gifts and then tell him that we don't want them? Isn't it a poor compliment to the goodness of the Creator, to regard his creatures as something evil?

Those are the terms of the debate, very crudely put. And, at least for a bother-headed person like myself, it is a perpetual source of worry trying to find out which party is in the right of it. The affirmative way seems so much easier to practise, the negative way so much easier to use as a standard of what is the better course to take in any given circumstances. On the one side, the negative people can point to a very strong tradition of ascetic theology which is for ever nagging at us about the austerities of the saints, as if these were the recognized blue-print of the ordinary Christian way of living—which opposes the Love of God to the love of creatures, with the implication that the more you have of one the less, ipso facto, you have of the other. Meanwhile, the affirmative people keep on telling you that some of us, including the saints, have a special vocation from God to serve him by renouncing, as far as possible, the use of creatures, but that this is only one way of serving him, and that the poet who tells us "He prayeth best, who loveth best / All creatures great and small" had got hold of an equally important, though less distinctively supernatural truth. Everybody admits that mortification is no use except in so far as it helps us to union with God; apart from that, it can only minister to our sinful pride. If, then, some people feel that it is easier to find God in creatures, and to approach him *through* creatures, why may not their way be as good as the other?

Well, let us first of all defend the negative people and remind ourselves that their attitude is not really a negative one. What they want is something positive, and what they renounce they renounce just because it stands between them and the positive thing they want, and just in so far as it stands between them and the positive thing they want. The characteristic type of asceticism in the early Church was what you might call a Benedictine type; you went away from the world. Ask some Father of the Desert why he lived such an uncomfortable life, and he would have told you, "I must get solitude; I must get silence; my soul has no room to breathe in the heavy atmosphere of the world." He didn't exactly want the discomforts of desert life; he wanted peace. And in the Middle Ages, the characteristic type of asceticism was what you might call Franciscan. Ask some early friar why he lived such a vagabond life, in such coarse clothes, with such simple food, and he would have told you, "I must get away from the ties, the restraints of common living; I can't think about God or my soul if I am always having to sign transfers of property and fill up income-tax returns." He didn't exactly want to sleep in hedgerows; he wanted freedom. At the Counter-Reformation, the characteristic type of asceticism was what you might call Jesuit; although perhaps in some ways you get a clearer picture of it from Saint John of the Cross than from Saint Ignatius. Ask either of those men why he valued such rigid discipline of the senses, and even of the thoughts, and he would have told you, "I have no time for anything which by-passes the main aim of my life, union with God"; he wanted love. Peace, freedom, love, it is always something positive that is the end in view.

Still the fact remains that the saints always have felt they were getting nearer God in proportion as they got further away from creatures—from their fellow-men, from riches and honours, from the busy interests which distract our thoughts. And here, I think, is where we make our mistake—we think of that process as if it were an automatic process. We imagine (if this is not too crude an illustration) the sort of thing which happens if you dip a tooth-glass into a basin, with the open end downwards, and then turn it slightly to one side. Some of the air escapes, and just the same amount of water comes in. And we imagine that if we could really make up our minds to get rid of some enjoyable thing in our lives, if we gave up smoking, for example, and if smoking represents, say, one-tenth of the enjoyment in our lives, the effect would be instantaneous. The Love of God is so pressing round our souls, trying to get in, that if we gave up one-tenth of the enjoyment in our lives, our lives would become one-tenth full of the Love of God. And of course they wouldn't. The first thing we should do would be to have a row with the man next door.

When you are told that, there's a temptation for you to make a mistake in the opposite direction. There's a temptation for you to sit back and say to yourself, "Good, that's all right. He means that it is the other way round. True mortification doesn't imply that we give up things to let the Love of God flow in; it means that the Love of God pushes in and drives the love of creatures out. So we haven't got to think about giving up anything or renouncing anything until the Love of God comes and does it for us." No, I'm afraid it isn't as simple as all that either. I imagine that if you could look into the heart of a saint, you would see the divine love which grants favours to the saint, and the human love which expresses itself in mortification, locked together in an interplay so close that you would not be able to tell which provoked which. For that is, surely, part of the mystery about this mysterious thing we call love. It is not the resultant of two complementary forces; it is, somehow, a single force. Its give and take is so spontaneous that you spend yourself in vain trying to determine which it is that gives, which that takes. Ah, if only our lives were on that level, at which the question, "Where the initiative comes from, seems to be meaningless!"

They aren't on that level. May I offer you rather a crude parallel to illustrate the situation we are in? Union with God is that happy harbour of the saints to which we are all aspiring, but the saints sail before a full wind astern; there is nothing left for them to do but to spread their canvas before it as wide as possible. We have to make our way against a head wind, and we do it by tacking. We make first one course, and then the direct opposite, and by this alternation we contrive, though only by little and little, to make headway. Now it is by the way of negation, by voluntarily making some sacrifice of time, or leisure, or comfort, or the amenities of our life to God, when circumstances seem to indicate it. Now it is by the way of affirmation, throwing ourselves into those harmless enjoyments which come our way, and doing our best to remember, all the time, our duty of conscious gratitude to him—trying, all the time, to see the Giver in his gifts, to reach the Giver through his gifts. We do that, almost instinctively, in the case of certain rather rarefied emotions; it is almost impossible to look at certain effects of scenery, for example, and I imagine to listen to certain kinds of music, if you are musical, without being forced beyond your appreciation of what your senses reveal, into a mood of adoration. And I think what the way of affirmation really means is, that if we would think a little more and learn to appreciate a little more, we should realize that about other things too, that every moment of lightheartedness we experience would serve to take us back to God.

The question obviously suggests itself, yes, but if we are to go tacking about like this, instead of having a straight course mapped out in front of us, how are we to be sure from day to day that we are doing the thing right, that we are not being pig-headed, not in danger of becoming swollen-headed, over the mortifications we do practise? And on the other side, that we are not simply letting ourselves have a good time, on the pretext that it makes us so splendidly grateful to God? Well, let me stick to my metaphor, or at any rate to one which is closely allied to it. A man who knows how to steer a boat, even if you blindfold him, can tell from the feel of the helm whether he is making just the best use of the wind he has got. If he is sailing just a bit too much into the wind or too much away from the wind he is conscious at once that the resistance of the tiller isn't right; I don't know the technical terms of the thing. And I fancy that if we stick to our prayer and learn a little skill in prayer we shall be just like that over the difficulty we have just been raising. We shall know instinctively when the rudder of our lives needs a bit of a twist to left or right.

But I know you will think I am trying to fob you off with generalizations; "Why can't he give us some *rules*?" is the thought uppermost in your minds. Well, if I try to descend into detail, I am afraid it won't take us very far, but I'll try to do the best I can. Here is one rule I would suggest: Do let us get more into the habit of thanking God for things. And especially for plain, simple things which we enjoy almost without knowing it, things like sandwiches in the train and putting on soft shoes after a hard day on your feet. That is, I think, one of the most delightful things about Saint Francis; his asceticism took the form, not so much of sighing and groaning over the luxuries of the world, as of making people see what a lot of simple pleasures they were missing. There is a very charming story of his sitting down with one of the brothers to have an al fresco meal on a journey, and getting quite enthusiastic about the shade of the trees they were sitting under; how thoughtful of Providence on a hot day like this to have given them a kind of roof over their heads! It is so terribly easy to forget to say thank you for God's gifts. If you want a simple formula for remembering to, I would suggest this—when you make your daily examination of conscience, make it in the form of working out your credit and debit account with Almighty God during the past twenty-four hours. Put it down, as it were, in parallel columns; "How has he been treating you, and how have I been treating him?" If you do that, you will necessarily find material for gratitude; and gratitude is, I think, the first foundation of any ascetic theology whatsoever.

Then here is another rule for the way of affirmation—whatever enjoyments we refuse in life, there is one kind of enjoyment we have got to accept if it's at all humanly possible; and that is the sort of enjoyment which is provided for us, out of deliberate kindness, by other people. You must be very, very far on in the state of union with God before you dare to refuse a present of home-grown peas from the man next door. There's a very deep-seated and very silly kind of pride in us which makes us instinctively want to say "No thank you", when we are offered the loan of an umbrella. It is much more to the point to mortify that kind of pride than to starve ourselves—much better to lick our lips over the home-grown peas than to wear peas in our shoes. And don't think that I am offering you lax counsel here. For this duty of charity towards our neighbour will involve us in a good many acceptances which we don't really very much enjoy; it will mean, sometimes, listening to a concert which we would have gone miles to avoid.

And now about rules for the way of negation. Here is a simple one, for times of retreat. Supposing a doctor had just told me I had only six months more to live, what changes would I now be introducing into my way of living? Some of those changes—not all, but some; common sense will tell you which—are worth introducing now.

Another simple rule—if you are looking about for some kind of sacrifice you can make for God, whether permanently, or just for the time being as a way of keeping Lent better, or something of that sort—ask yourself whether there isn't one which incidentally would remove from you the occasions of sin. If you are given to uncharitable talk, for instance, the right mortification for you is silence. I wonder why nobody except the religious ever thinks of silence as a possible means of mortification? If your faults mostly spring from physical laziness, ration your use of the armchair. Be *practical* in your asceticism; don't aspire to become the sort of piebald saint who sleeps on a board and is not on speaking terms with his sister-in-law.

But the best rule of all is to watch your prayer, and ask yourself honestly whether your prayer is being interfered with by the sort of amusements which occupy your spare time. Such and such a friendship is perfectly innocent and reasonable; but does the memory of it, often recurring to your mind, distract you at your prayer, or does it bring you closer to God? You have a hobby of some kind, a very good thing to have. But are you letting it get the better of you so that you spend over it some of the time which you know you ought to be giving to prayer? You are fond of reading, or fond of taking exercise; are you sure that you don't sometimes tire yourself out with these recreations in such a way as to make the effort of prayer come more difficult to you? Don't be scrupulous about this; the effort of prayer comes difficult to all of us, and it is ten to one that if you got rid of this particular distraction you would only get another instead. But make sure that you are not so ordering your life as to keep God at arm's length, as to make a kind of cushion between yourself and the thought of eternity.

And finally, though it's almost too obvious to be worth stating, there is one test which you must be constantly applying, the test of efficiency. The thing which comes first is your job. You are not a statue standing on a pillar; you are a cog in a machine. And when I talk about your job, I don't mean simply the means by which you earn your bread, or the work which you do directly for the glory of God. I mean all the complex of social relations which make up your life. It is part of your job to be kind to other people, not to squash them, to cheer them up, not to depress them. The kind of self-denial God certainly does ask of you is the kind of self-denial that will make you more useful to your fellow-men. And the kind of self-denial he certainly does not ask of you is the kind of self-denial which will turn you into a prig or a wet blanket or a nervous wreck. You don't want to follow the way of affirmation in such a degree as to make people think, "What a good time these Christians have!"—and people are very ready to think that. You don't want to follow the way of negation in such a degree as to make people think, "Well, I'm glad I'm not a Christian, if that is the kind of person Christians are." You mustn't try to force your nature into a wholly different pattern; you must be what God made you, only trying to make of it what God meant you to make of it—your hand always lying light on the tiller, ready to catch any breath of guidance that God will send you.

XIX

ON GOOD NATURE

Have you ever considered what a curious phrase it is we use, when we call one of our friends "good-natured"?

Theologically speaking, our language is of course inaccurate, and indeed heretical. The good-natured people who have existed in the world can be counted on the fingers of one hand: our Blessed Lady, of course, and Saint John the Baptist, and possibly the prophet Jeremiah; who else? And at the same time, if we are using language quite loosely, why should the words "good-natured" be a rare compliment which we bestow on one or two people here and there? What about all the other people? Why aren't they good-natured? What's to prevent them? Why do we find ourselves saying, "I do admire Smith; he's so good-natured"? It's as if we were to say, "I do admire Smith; he's nearly six feet high."

Very often, when we pay people such a tribute, we mean that they are different from ourselves. They do willingly, instinctively, with a good grace, the ordinary polite or kindly things which you only do after laborious consideration, which entirely spoils the doing of them. If somebody says, "Would you care to come out for a walk?" it is the signal for great searchings of heart on your part; shall you or shall you not? The work you are doing at the moment isn't the least bit important, the least bit attractive; the weather is fine; a walk might quite possibly do you good—all those things have to be thought out, and at last you say, "Oh, well, all right", as if you were conferring a great favour on him. And then you say to somebody, "Would you care to come out for a walk?" and he says, "Right! Splendid! I must just go up and put on my shoes; I'll be down in a couple of minutes." And you find yourself reflecting what a good-natured person he is, and wondering why you are not.

I dare say all that sounds frivolous, but I'm not sure that it is. The same differences of temperament betray themselves, don't they, over more important matters than going out for an afternoon walk. It may be a matter of sending a subscription to a charity, it may be a matter of rescuing somebody who has fallen into a canal, it may be a matter of warning a friend about dangerous habits, dangerous company, which might prove to be the ruin of him; how one person's reactions differ from another's, how much quicker off the mark A is than B! And the question I am always posing to myself is this: Is it better to do the right thing, even when you are sure it is the right thing, spontaneously, by instinct? Or cautiously, deliberately, after weighing up all your motives in the sight of Almighty God?

Put it like that to the ordinary person you meet, and the answer will be, "Oh, the first way for me, every time!" After all, he argues, if you were a beggar, and asked for the price of a night's lodging, which would you rather meet? The donor who simply says, "What, no money? How absolutely rotten!" and produces the sum immediately? Or the donor who says, "Well, as a matter of fact I can't really afford it, but perhaps as it's my wife's birthday I might stretch a point"? After all, our Lord himself says that when you bestow alms your left hand oughtn't to know what your right hand is doing; surely that means that he approves of the uncalculating gift? And certainly from the natural point of view I think we all do admire the unreflective character. The care-free, slapdash sort of person who blunders through the world rather creditably, doing a good deal of harm and guilty, now and again, of moral lapses, how ready we are to pardon him! After all (we say) he is so good-natured. He has the defects of his qualities; what is a mistake here, even a fault there, in one who faces life so freely and fearlessly, takes everything in his stride?

But that, you see, brings us right up against the doctrine of intention. I am sure you have all read before now the kind of pious book which has a whole chapter, at the very least, on the subject of intention. Most of our actions, when all is said and done, are of themselves indifferent; brushing your hair, or reading a novel, or playing a round of golf, isn't something right or something wrong. Has it, therefore, no value? On the contrary, say the spiritual authors, every action has a moral value; it depends on the intention with which it is performed. Brushing your hair out of mere vanity is wrong; reading a novel out of mere curiosity is at the best a waste of time; playing golf in order to boast afterwards about how well you putted is sinful pride. All these things, daily actions that have to be got through, harmless recreations which make us come back to our work with more zest, are good actions if they are performed consciously, to the glory of Almighty God.

Now, where does your care-free hero get off, if that is the right doctrine? If he always appears to act without thinking, how can we suppose that he is directing his intention properly? Even his good actions, when he throws his money about or goes out of his way to play with the children, to spare a kind word for some humble person whom everybody else neglects—are we certain that they are really *good* actions? That he does them with any kind of moral intention, and not from mere thoughtless bonhomie which (according to the spiritual authors) gets you nowhere? After all, as a matter of common experience, these splendid people we call good-natured have, often enough, no kind of religion, no attitude even towards religion. They aren't even stuffy atheists; they just don't seem to bother about eternity or anything of that kind. Can we really suppose that the spiritual authors approve of them?

Well, we can be content to leave them in God's hands; but we have to think about ourselves, about the way in which our own lives are going to be mapped out, in full consciousness of the destiny that depends on them. How are we going to set about it? Are we going to spend a lot of our time in prayer forming intentions about this and that, directing our intentions to this or that end? Are we going to make a lightning meditation on eternity every time we hear the clock strike? Are we determined never to go to bed without having warned at least one Christian soul of its dangers? Are we going to make a point of offering up, there and then, all our mortifications and set-backs? Are we going to make a formal act of humility every time we hear anything said in our praise? In a word, are we going to put force on ourselves all the while, consciously drill ourselves into all that we think the spiritual authors would like us to be?

Or, what is the alternative? I suppose, to be ourselves. It is possible, I mean, just to go on saying our prayers, making our morning offering and committing, in general, all our intentions to God, asking him to use them for his glory, and then muddle along, rather anyhow—trying, of course, to keep in the presence of God, and to beware of the obvious temptations, but being ourselves all the time, reacting naturally to situations, trusting divine grace and Divine Providence to make the best of it, to make the best of our very inadequate attempts to do the right thing, say the right thing, as we see the opportunity coming along.

Which is it to be? I suppose in the long run it is a question of what we think about nature and grace. We all know that our nature is injured by the Fall, and we all know that it isn't wholly corrupted by the Fall. But what do we feel in our bones about it? That's the point. I'm bound to say I think the whole tradition of Christian spirituality tends to paint our nature very black indeed. That's partly owing to the Fathers of the Desert, partly to Saint Augustine. If you read between the lines of the *Imitation of Christ*—and I suppose anybody would name that as typical, safe Christian spirituality—you will find that our fallen nature really gets a very poor show; we must be always fighting it, always contradicting it, at every moment, or we shall start rolling downhill in no time.

All that is true, and yet we know that it is possible to exaggerate the fallenness of our nature; that is really why the Church quarrelled with the Jansenists. To be sure, there were notions of abstract theology involved; but the real trouble about the Jansenists wasn't their notions of abstract theology; it was their attitude to the very living, practical question "How much is the Fall going to make pessimists of us?" If you take a woman like Mère Angélique, the Abbess of Port Royal, very holy in her way but a dreadful old woman, I think, you will see that she hardly makes any allowance for our having any right instincts and saving qualities at all. By her way of it, you must do everything scrupulously for the Love of God, with no trace of any other motive in your actions. If you give money to a beggar you must be sure that it is from Love of God, not out of any pity for the beggar—that would be "concupiscence". But in real life, of course, if you said to the beggar, "I dislike your looks intensely, and this penny is being bestowed on you entirely for the Love of God, and not because I am in the least bit sorry for you", he would throw it back in your face—and quite right too.

It doesn't do; you can't go on splitting things up like that; you lose contact with real life. Do you remember the story about a Father of the Desert, I forget which, who was given a lovely bunch of grapes? And all the monks stood round watching to see what edifying reactions he would have about it. What he did was devour them greedily, all of them, in front of the astonished community, and explain afterwards that he had been mortifying the sinful pride which would have urged him to refuse them. I can't believe that we were ever meant to sort out our motives with that kind of barren meticulousness; it only leads you into a mass of scruple and unreality.

Must all our actions be done consciously and deliberately, there and then, out of love for God and with a conscious intention of promoting his glory? Are we to say that any action which doesn't fulfil those conditions is wasted, if not worse, perhaps is sinful, as Saint Augustine makes out that all the good works of the heathen are sinful? It really looks as if it were time we tried to find out what our Lord himself taught about it. What is the passage we are invited to look up in that connexion? Probably the parable of the Ten Virgins, at the beginning of the twenty-fifth chapter of Saint Matthew. The Jansenist points you gleefully to this story, and says, "There you are! Ten virgins, all virgins, but only five of them were thinking about the Love of God—that is what the oil means. And the other five, who weren't thinking about the Love of God, came too late for the queue." I know, it looks as if the question were decided. But just turn to the end of the chapter, the same chapter.

There you get that terrific account of the Last Judgement, at which the Good Shepherd will divide the sheep from the goats. He will say to the people on his right hand, "All the kindness you did to the most insignificant of my brethren here, you did to me. What's that you say? You weren't thinking about me? You'd never heard of me? That's not the point. The point is that that scoundrel over there was sent to prison, and you were sorry for the poor fellow and went to try and cheer him up—you admit that? Very well, then; you did it to me." I don't see how our Lord could possibly have declared himself more definitely on the opposite side, just when we thought we had got his teaching taped for good and all.

We seem to be plunged in worse difficulties than ever. But let me remind you that the account of the Last Judgement doesn't follow immediately on the parable of the Ten Virgins; there are seventeen verses in between. And what are they about? About the king who went off on a journey, leaving each of his servants so many talents to do business with. Now, if you like to insist that these talents refer exclusively to divine grace, and have nothing to do with the natural order at all, I'm afraid we are back where we were. But I am sure Saint Chrysostom is right; you cannot limit the parable like that. It refers not only to the graces we receive, but to our natural gifts as well, our "talents", as we call them, in allusion to this parable. Now, here as in the other two parts of the chapter, we are concerned with judgement; but the judgement, this time, is awarded, it seems, on a different principle.

With the sheep and the goats, the important question was, "What did you do?" With the Ten Virgins it was, "In what spirit did you do it?" Here the question is, "What growth have you to show? When I went away and left you, apparently at least, to your own devices, I gave each of you a little nest-egg. Not the same to each, and I am not expecting the same returns from each. But has there been growth on your own lines? Are there any more eggs in the nest? Have you improved your opportunities, developed your capabilities? If so, the feast; if not, the darkness."

Isn't that, perhaps, the solution of our difficulties? There *is* good in our natures; it's all very well for the *Imitation* to say that it's only a miserable spark hidden away among the embers, but it's there, it's real. In each of us, the Fall has warped it somehow, but not always in the same way or in the same direction. Human nature is not a constant thing; it's not the same in everybody; and we shall be judged, not by what we might have done if we had been somebody different, but by what we did, being what we were.

Very well, you say, then that's quite clear; each of us ought to follow the line of his own nature, make the best of the temperament God has given him, develop it to the utmost. If God has made me an easy-going person, it is by that path I must serve him; if he has made me a toiler and a plodder, I must toil and plod—well, to tell the truth, that wasn't what I was going to say. I was going to say just the opposite.

Some people are by nature exuberant; they run to extremes; they act on the spur of the moment; their sympathies, their passions, are easily aroused. Conventions, engagements, rubrics, sit lightly on them; they take everything in their stride. They look on the bright side of things; every second person they come across they describe as a "splendid fellow", without being quite certain of recognizing him when they next meet. Others are by nature wizened, cautious, introspective; their instinct is always to think twice and then to do nothing. They are conscientious to a fault; an unpaid bill, an unanswered letter, haunts them like a nightmare. Their difficulty is to open up, to throw themselves into things; they hesitate, calculate, and opportunity passes them by. Am I wrong in thinking, that if you are to make the best of the temperament God has endowed you with, he means you to counteract its bias, to strain it in the opposite direction? The spiritual authors, after all, know what they are talking about when they encourage us to practise mortification. The Wise Virgins trimmed their lamps. A lamp untrimmed is almost as bad as a lamp with no oil in it.

If, then, you are the sort of happy-go-lucky person whom the world calls "good-natured", then your nature wants watching; and probably it will need a few rules, irritating and cramping in themselves, while you are about it. I don't mean that you are to start forming intentions; I'm sure Almighty God didn't mean us, didn't mean any of us, to spend half our lives forming intentions. No, but I'll tell you the kind of thing I mean, the only kind of thing I mean. Possibly you are a bit of a chatterbox, a bit indiscreet. Your friends, perhaps, before now have performed their duty of fraternal correction by pointing that out to you. Well, you can't be always riding yourself on the curb. But there may be special occasions when you want to be extra careful; there will be non-Catholics about, or there will be touchy people about, or for some reason the going will be sticky. Well, there's no harm on occasions like that of having a rule that you will count ten before you speak. *That* won't destroy your liberty of spirit.

If and in so far as you have the opposite temperament, the wizened, cautious, diffident temperament, it is very doubtful if rules were meant for you. If you do try to live by rules at all, let them be such as to counteract your poverty of nature, not such as to drive it deeper in. Some of us, I think, might do well to have this rule, where no sin or scandal is concerned; always go by your first thought, and disregard the second. Somebody asks you to go out for a walk, and you think, "Well, it is rather a fine day"—*shoot*! Say yes, at once; don't stop to think about the letters you have to write. You meet somebody unexpectedly, or get a sudden opening in conversation which prompts you to put in a word in season, a word embarrassing to say, but calculated perhaps to save a soul from taking a wrong turning; say it; don't stop to think of all the reasons for not saying it. That, let me tell you, is heroic advice; very few people are capable of profiting by it.

XX

ON MINOR TRIALS

I want to talk to you about those surprising words of our Lord after the Feeding of the Five Thousand: "Gather up the broken pieces that are left over, so that nothing may be wasted."

Surprising, I call them, because after all you would have expected our Blessed Lord to be a man careless of detail. If you are going to divide up human beings into two classes, one of the most obvious lines of demarcation is between the people who do things on the grand scale and people who do things with laborious accuracy—impressionists, you may call them, and Pre-Raphaelites; the Impressionist will produce his whole effect with a few strokes of the brush; the Pre-Raphaelite will spend laborious hours etching in tiny points of detail. As in art, so in life; how one envies the man who can rule a country, or control the world's markets, by mere dash and brilliancy, getting all the donkey-work done by a host of subordinates nobody ever hears of! How one admires the research student who sits down, day after day, to his interminable calculations, adding in some imperceptible degree, after a life-time of it, to the general sum of human knowledge! And it is a matter of temperament, you feel; each is working in his own way, and if you made them exchange jobs, either would make a hash of it. I have found myself, before now, dividing up Mass-servers into two classes, the pourers and the tricklers. The pourer gives you the ablutions in half the time, but once in a while he makes a false move and sends a tidal wave of water up your sleeve; the trickler never does that. Everybody has his qualities; everybody has the defects of his qualities, and you mustn't expect too much of one person.

Now, when our Lord Jesus Christ became man, he became a man, this particular man, belonging, therefore, to certain divisions of the human race, and not to others. He was a man, not a woman, a Jew, not a Greek or a Roman, he was of such and such a height, his eyes were of such and such a colour, he belonged to a particular blood-group. Naturally, then, we should assume that he fell into one or other of the two divisions I have just been trying to indicate to you. Was he, we ask, the sort of man who moves through life making splendid gestures, which rivet the attention and capture the hearts of his fellow men, leaving them to fill in the dull details afterwards? Or was he the sort of man who secures his results by paying enormous attention to detail, weighing every step, calculating the exact effect of every utterance, punctual, and tidy, and thrifty with the honourable thrift of the poor?

We think we know the answer; of course he was the first kind of man! Surely, if there was ever a man who did things in a big way, it was Jesus of Nazareth! "If any man comes to me, without hating his father and mother and children and brethren and sisters, yes, and his own life too, he can be no disciple of mine"; those are his authentic accents, demanding all or nothing. He will heal all the sick that lie around him, not just single out the deserving cases; he will turn out all the traders from the Temple, whip in hand, not stop to consider whether one or two may not have some business to be there. His disciples are not to look forward and plan for the future; the future will look after itself; they are to go out staff in hand, with no reserves of food or of clothes, trusting to what they can pick up on the way. The message they preach is to be a take-it-or-leave-it affair; if they can't get a hearing, they must shake off the dust of this city and try the next. If they get into trouble with magistrates, they are to say just what comes into their heads, not make up long speeches in self-defence. The whole thing is to be a reckless adventure; there is to be no counting of the cost, except for that preliminary computation which assures them that if a man loses the whole world to achieve the salvation of his own soul, it is worth it.

That is the kind of man Jesus of Nazareth was, we say, a man who thought in thousands, not in pennies. And when you come to think of it, what could be more natural? Wasn't he up against the Pharisees, miserable higglers and sticklers about tiny points of the Law? The people who were for ever taking tithes of mint and anise and dill, approaching life in the spirit of a chemist making up some very exact formula, in which a hair's-breadth mistake would be fatal. The people who were quite ready to forgive their brother seven times, if they could be certain of getting their own back on him the eighth, who were quite ready to show mercy to their neighbour, as long as it could be proved that he did really come from the same village, and wasn't a comparative stranger. The people who were always straining at a gnat and swallowing a camel, bothering about whether you might pay tribute to Caesar, and how far you could walk without sin on the sabbath day, instead of wondering why the poor man at their gates was so badly off, and whether something couldn't be done about it. No wonder if our Lord, in the splendid honesty of his nature, reacted against all that kind of thing. "Don't worry about what exactly constitutes murder; stop hating one another! Don't take a lawyer's opinion to see exactly how much compensation you can get out of the men who stole your overcoat; throw your coat after it, and say *Here, take that*!" It wasn't so much the pride of the Pharisees, or their heartlessness, or their stinginess, that our Lord complained of; it was the dreadful niggling way they went about it. His whole life, his whole teaching, is a continual protest, if you like to put it in that way, against the pettifogging meticulousness of his contemporaries.

And we are apt to think of his two great nature-miracles as a kind of signature-tune which expresses the magnificence, the carelessness of gesture with which our Lord threw down his defiance to the world around him. At Cana of Galilee, it isn't quite clear whether he made the whole well run wine instead of water, or simply stored up wine in the six water-pots—that would be about eighty gallons of wine, to supply the needs of a single country wedding! The point is in either case that there was no stint—no pause for reflexion, as if he were considering how much would be good for the guests—and the same with this miracle of the Five Thousand; it wasn't, perhaps, absolutely necessary, they were not quite beyond the reach of bakers' shops. But he isn't going to worry about the bakers' shops: "Oh, don't stand there arguing whether two hundred pennyworth of bread would be just enough or just not enough; how much have we got? Five loaves? Very well, that'll be all right; make the men sit down." And they all ate, and were filled; nor was that all. As they moved off down the hill-side, there was bread lying about everywhere; no, don't say "crumbs"—our Lord wasn't conducting an anti-litter campaign, he wasn't worrying about the amenities of Transjordan. No, great hunks of bread, which people had taken in the first instance and then left lying about for fear they should be sick if they ate any more—that's what the "fragments" were. Here, as at Cana of Galilee, grace abounded—so much more provided than anybody could possibly want! And we said to ourselves, "Here is the authentic Son of God! See what profusion, what apparent waste there is everywhere in the world God has created! So, when the Son of God comes to earth, he is not limited by his materials; he does things on a big scale, never stops (why should he?) to worry about the details."

And then, what an anti-climax! Goodness, how he lets us down! "Gather up the broken pieces that are left over", exactly as if they were a set of school-boys after a picnic! "Here, Bartholomew, there's a big piece just beyond you you haven't noticed!" He does care, after all, about the odd pence—does want us to pay attention to those inconsiderable details. These are the very men who are to go out preaching without so much as a wallet between them; and here they are, each with his wallet, gathering up hunks of bread, twelve baskets full. They have been told never to exercise themselves about the morrow, and here they are hoarding up scraps in case they should come in useful. The men that should have been converting a world, set down to clear away after the meal! What does it all mean?

It means, I suppose, that you and I have got Jesus Christ wrong. We thought of him, instinctively, as sharing all our human limitations, and therefore as having the defects of his qualities; but he hasn't any defects. There is nothing really fine, really splendid, about waste. We only admire wastefulness when and because it is combined with a certain generosity of character. We saw that generosity of character in Jesus Christ, and we assumed that he would be wasteful about trifling things, as generous people so often are. We forgot that he was perfect.

And perhaps that paradox in our Lord's attitude towards life is meant to encourage you and me when we are got down by what you may call the pettiness of the Christian life as it is ordinarily lived. There is a kind of vanity in us, a kind of restlessness in us, which makes us want to feel that we are doing things in a big way; and religion, being the biggest thing of all, ought to give us that feeling more than anything else—but it doesn't. It seems to be a happy hunting-ground for the pious souls that like to go round collecting indulgences, two hundred days here and a quarantine or two there; it seems to suit the mental requirements of people who like liturgy and spend a lot of time looking up the book of instructions to make sure that they don't say the commemorations at Vespers back to front. But above all, what strikes us is the insignificance, the unimpressiveness, of the day-to-day sacrifice we make to our Blessed Lord. When we receive absolution, the priest says, "May the merits of the Blessed ever-Virgin Mary and all the saints, and all the good thou hast done, all the ill thou hast suffered, avail thee for the remission of sins." All the good *I* have done, all the ill *I* have suffered—that's a good laugh, you say, in your mood of self-abasement. Think what it must have been like living in the first centuries of the Christian religion, or even in England at the time of the persecutions; think of what it means, now, being a Catholic anywhere east of Berlin, compared with being a Catholic anywhere west of Berlin! How can I talk of myself as offering any sacrifice to our Lord at all? Perhaps some of us, in the war years, have known what it was to be surrounded by hardships and dangers; all that lies behind us, and the world has gone rather flat. With the more urgency does the question present itself, What sacrifice am I offering to our Lord now?

It is at such times of disillusionment that we can comfort ourselves with his words: "Gather up the broken pieces that are left over, so that nothing may be wasted." He, with all the economy of a universe passing between his hands, is not too busy to look after the scraps. And indeed, for fear we should be blind to that, for fear we should lose sight of that, he has given us a Saint in our own times whose characteristic message is that a lifetime of small endurances may, through his grace and by his Providence, be a life of exceptional spiritual achievement. That is the revelation which makes Saint Thérèse of Lisieux still, in the best sense, popular. It is not a question of miracles; it is not a question of gaudy statues and pretty-pretty devotions. The reason why people still listen to Saint Thérèse of Lisieux is because she taught us that heroic sanctity does not mean, necessarily, doing heroic things.

That's easily said. But once you set about reducing that principle to practice, it isn't so easy. What permanent attitude towards the minor setbacks of life are you and I going to adopt, so as to get the greatest possible spiritual profit out of them and at the same time avoid turning ourselves into most appalling prigs? Our life is so largely made up, isn't it, of small, undignified set-backs. You miss your train, you have indigestion, the electric light is cut off when you are in the middle of shaving, boring people drop in to see you and won't go, the handle comes off the drawer you are trying to open, and the bank's shut because it's early-closing day—all sorts of little things like that. Pinpricks, all of them; but if you knelt down at night and tried to remember all your grievances instead of remembering your sins, it would keep you half an hour on your knees. Perhaps one day, when your luck has been out worse than usual, you retail a list of these mishaps to the tobacconist's wife at the corner. There is no kind of doubt what she will say; it is a stereotyped formula. She will put on her most comforting look, and say, "Ah, well, Sir, these things are sent to try us, aren't they?" One of those bits of theology which have got stuck in the English mind; and what a dreadful bit of theology! These things are sent, that is, sent by Almighty God, and for a purpose. His purpose is to put us on our trial, and to judge us by seeing, from moment to moment, how we react to the test. Instead of comforting us, the old lady's explanation is calculated to make us run shrieking from the shop.

Well, what *is* our attitude going to be? I am not trying to lay down the law; I am quite honestly exposing the hesitations of my own mind. It is possible, no doubt, to take a strictly theological line about it—to fall down on your knees when the light goes out while you are shaving, and tell Almighty God that you have deserved this punishment by your sins, and that you are prepared if need be to go on in darkness all the rest of your life, to show your love for him. When I say that, you complain that I am making the whole thing sound silly and high-falutin' and exaggerated. Well, of course I am; I'm just trying out a formula, and obviously it doesn't quite add up. No, there are certain major discomforts in life, prolonged and wearing to the patience, which you can, I think, offer up to God without losing your sense of proportion, a toothache, for example, or a sleepless night. I don't think there's anything ludicrous about offering up a sleepless night for the holy souls—it seems the natural thing to do. But the difficulty comes in with these tiny, undignified set-backs like breaking your shoe-lace suddenly or stepping in a puddle or something of that kind, the things that make you want to swear. Is it possible, without losing your sense of proportion, without enveloping your religion in an atmosphere of unreality, to be always offering those things up? Most of us would say not. Most of us would say, "Take it all in your stride; try to get into the habit of saying something milder than the word you meant to say; and, after all, if you are in a state of grace, there must be some whiff of merit in the thing; let us be content with that."

I know, but I am still haunted by that phrase of the tobacconist's wife: "These things are sent to try us." There must be a right religious reaction to this infinite series of infinitesimal annoyances which is the web and woof of our daily lives. And I think the instinct which makes us react wrong is a sort of pride: "How is it that I, who have done nothing to deserve it, should have had such a run of bad luck at bridge?" It's a kind of personal affront; and I suppose that is why missing a train when there are porters watching is so much worse than missing the train when there are no porters watching. If that's so, the right reaction isn't precisely one of self-oblation, but one of humility. I am going to put this awfully badly, but I think if you and I were a good deal holier people than we are, I mean, than I am, the effect of each little absurd contretemps would be to plunge us deeper in the sense of our own nothingness. There's a kind of interior act of self-obliteration, of lying doggo and pretending to the devil that you aren't there, which does really, I think, meet the case. You know they say that a man doesn't hurt himself falling over if only he will have the presence of mind to keep his muscles slack, instead of tightening them. In the same way, I think, what makes us come badly out of the test when these things are sent to try us is our first reaction of pride—that this collar-stud should be trying to escape from *me*!—and if we can ju-jitsu away this first reaction of pride, there's almost nothing we can't do in the way of sanctifying our set-backs.

Please forgive me if I seem to have wasted half-an-hour of your recollection-time in talking about trifles. They are trifles, of course, but I think the longer you live the more you become conscious of great tracts of your life which seem simply wasted, like a hill-side covered with crusts of bread which ought to have found their way into somebody's satchel. It's not only the discomforts and the disappointments, of course; what a lot of opportunities we miss in life by never being thankful for small mercies! We ought to offer up the pleasant moments of life too; and when I had to look after school-girls, and the nuns encouraged them to make up spiritual bouquets in which they registered a list of sacrifices, I always insisted that if the bouquet was for me it should have a list of so many ice-creams eaten and so many visits made to the cinema for my intention. But on the whole it is the uncomfortable things that stick out most; and on the whole what gets you down most, as you look back over the flat, arid levels of day-to-day existence, is the interminable record of the little things that were sent to try you, and found you wanting.

XXI

LIBERTY OF THE SPIRIT IN PRAYER

It seems a very simple subject—saying one's prayers; but as a matter of fact there is a great deal to be said about it, and there are so many different pathways for discussion that it's not easy to treat the subject without seeming to be, and perhaps being, disconnected. I want to suggest to you, at the start, one leading idea which is the idea that underlies all I am going to say. What I am really going to talk about is the liberty of the spirit. And that means—what? Let us put it, to start with, in an almost exaggerated, almost paradoxical form; then we will explain and qualify afterwards. The liberty of the spirit means that when you have to decide about the manner in which you will approach Almighty God in prayer, the best way to please him is to please yourself.

Prayer means—what? It means talking to God. We are apt to think that it means asking God for things; and so in a sense it does. We are all beggars, all down-and-outs, and we can't come before God, who is the giver of all things, without reminding ourselves and at the same time reminding him that we want something, want a whole lot of things. Even the most generous prayer of the most unselfish of saints is a kind of hint. But we mustn't, for that reason, imagine that Almighty God's attitude towards you and me, when we come to him in prayer, is the sort of attitude you and I take up towards a beggar in the street—usually, if the truth must be told, crossing to the other side of the street. You get a far more accurate picture of what our prayers mean to

Almighty God—though of course it can't be a quite accurate picture—if you think of a father who has come home with a present for his little son, knowing that it is what his son wants, but waiting to be asked for it. It's all wrapped up in brown paper and tucked away under the table, waiting to be asked for. And when we say that the father wants to be asked for it, we don't mean that he expects his son to have spent the whole day working up polite speeches out of a manual of etiquette, so as to put his request in a proper form. He wants his son to come and talk to him quite naturally; "Daddy, did you bring back anything for me from town?" will do as well as anything else. And Almighty God wants you and me to ask for his gifts naturally, in our own way, approaching him easily and confidently—not like the street beggar with his long rigmarole of petition.

We lose sight of that, because we obstinately cling to the idea that religion is meant to be an uncomfortable business, and no kind of religious exercise which doesn't make us thoroughly uncomfortable can be worth having. Well, of course there is such a thing as mortification; but I'm sure we aren't meant to go about our prayers in that sort of spirit. We aren't meant to choose the most uncomfortable time of day, and put ourselves into the most uncomfortable attitude, and say the longest possible prayers in the most rhetorical words we can possibly find, as if we were going to get what we want by deserving it. Prayer, even if it does mean asking God for things, doesn't mean trying to force God to give us things through our own efforts. We are to go to him easily and naturally, like children.

You see, it's all very well, but in this matter of prayer you and I labour under a frightful disability. When Adam and Eve were turned out of Paradise, what do you suppose was the first thing they noticed that had gone wrong? Surely they had distractions in their prayer; they had never had those before. It had all been plain sailing; now, they had to set to and say their prayers laboriously. All the thorns and briars he came across in his gardening didn't grow so rankly or so obstinately as the distractions in poor Adam's prayer. Ever since then you and I, his children, have been fighting a losing battle against distractions; saying prayers is a thing that goes against the grain with us at the best of times; and if we go out of our way to make it more difficult for ourselves, by praying in a forced and cramped way that doesn't come natural to us, obviously we are being foolish, and to tell the truth we are being rather conceited. I think I am right in saying, Saint Francis of Sales teaches us that if we find we pray best lying down, it is our job to pray lying down. We ought to say the prayers we like, not the prayers which we find rhetorical or sentimental or tedious, in the circumstances in which we can pray best, not in circumstances which hardly allow us to pray at all. Being such weak performers as we are, at least let us claim the liberty of the spirit.

Well, let's talk first of all about public prayer and see how this principle applies to that. The Church commands us to hear Mass on Sundays and holidays, that is, to be personally present while and where it is being celebrated. Strictly speaking, you fulfil that obligation even if you are reading a newspaper all the time; I think the theologians say you hear Mass even if you go to sleep at it, as long as you wake up for the Consecration. But evidently the Church means us to do something better than that, both on Sundays and feast days when we have to be there, and on other days when we go there as a matter of devotion. What ought we to be doing while Mass is going on? Surely we ought to be saying our prayers as best we can, and that means we ought to be saying our prayers in the way that suits us best, ought to be saying our prayers on any given morning in the way that suits us best that particular morning. I always get into trouble for saying this, but I shall go on saying it. There are a lot of good people going about who will give you to understand that it is your duty, your actual duty, to follow the words of the Mass while it is being said, and if you don't know Latin, to follow them in a Latin-English missal. I would agree, following the words of the Mass is an admirable way of occupying your time in Church; there could be none better—but always, I would say, with two provisos. The first is that you should find it does suit you, does help you to lift up your heart to God. And the second is, that you should find it still suits you; you have been doing it, year in, year out, for some time, and the consecrated words have lost, for you, the magic of novelty. Or haven't they? If they haven't, by all means go on. But if you are beginning to find it tedious, after all these years, it is possible—I don't say it is certain, but it is possible—that you would be the better for a change. To sit there doing nothing all through the Mass, simply waiting for it to be over—that, evidently, would be a tragic mistake. But to say your own prayers, with a book or without a book, with or without regard to what the priest is saying at the moment, is the best thing for you, if you feel that it meets best, for you, the spiritual needs of the moment.

And now let's come back to your own prayers. If liberty of spirit means anything, the important point about your own prayers is that they should be your own prayers. I mean, of course, that you should say them because you choose to say them—not because you think it is the thing to do, not because you have bound yourself by some kind of promise to say them and don't feel quite certain it wouldn't be a sin to leave them unsaid. Societies and sodalities and pious movements of every kind which make you undertake to say the De profundis every second Wednesday and so on—I haven't a word against them, God forbid I should have, if they are really being useful to you—if the prayers and the pious observances which they involve carry you along with them and are not a mere drudgery which you have got to get through somehow because you said you would. I am not telling you that you shouldn't join things of that sort; I am only saying that I hope you will be careful about it, and not say "Oh yes, rather, I'll join" in some rash moment because some friend of yours is pressing you to rally round. As far as possible, our prayers ought to be something we look forward to, not something we have got to get through. And nothing helps so much, I think, to give us that ungracious feeling about them, as a whole lot of prayer obligations, undertaken in haste and repented at leisure.

And of course there's another way in which the piety of our friends can involve us, if we are not careful, in weariness and scruple—I mean, when they say "Pray for me, won't you?" and leave us wondering whether we have promised, by saying yes, to go on praying for them for the rest of our lives. I think it's one of the things you first notice, if you are a convert, after your conversion—the way in which Catholic people are always asking one another for prayers, even on the slightest occasion. Somebody is going in for an examination, and you must help them to defeat the examiners; somebody is trying to find a house, and you must second the efforts of the house-agent, and so on. It is a lovely habit, this, which you had hardly experienced at all in your earlier days; not that non-Catholics don't pray for one another, but they are shy of asking for prayers, unless something has gone terribly wrong. And of course there are the mortuary cards that make their pathetic appeal to you at the church door; "Of your charity ... Of your charity"—dear me, how terribly lacking in charity I must be, to remember these people so seldom! Nothing could be more right, nothing could be more salutary; only, with some of us it does lead to scruple. We add ever fresh names to the list we mention in our daily prayers, and it gets longer and longer and more out of date; we find ourselves still praying for the recovery of somebody we met yesterday, in rude health, or for the special intentions of somebody whose name we remember vaguely but we can't quite remember who they are. I think I've read somewhere that if you asked Saint Francis of Assisi to pray for you, he knelt down and did it there and then; it would have been like him—he hated, didn't he, taking thought for the morrow. What I'm suggesting is that we ought, every now and again, to have a spring cleaning of our prayers, cutting out, as it were, the dead wood. Otherwise they become a kind of jungle that we have to hack our way through before we go to bed, and we come before God all wearied and worried, instead of throwing ourselves into his arms, as Christians should, and telling him what we really want.

Our prayers ought to be our own prayers, not only in the things we ask for but in our manner of asking; they should be natural, spontaneous, part of ourselves. I don't mean that we oughtn't to have regular times for them; most of us find that if we don't have regular times for them they drop out altogether. I don't mean that we oughtn't to use fixed forms of prayer, or favourite books which we use as a starting-point for our meditations. But the simpler they are, the better; don't let us feel proud of using long rhetorical sentences, or of pious aspirations which we don't really mean—as, for example, a desire for martyrdom. God wants us to be ourselves; he knows the kind of people we are, and, as I say, he knows the kind of things we want; we must go to him as a Father, who understands us, not treat him as if we were trying to put across a difficult message to somebody who was rather deaf and rather stupid. Never, for instance, repeat a prayer which you have already said, on the ground that you aren't sure whether you said it with sufficient attention. He knows all about that; he knows that you were tired, or bothered, or just simply that you were wool-gathering; tell him often that your prayers are a miserable failure, but don't repeat them.

When I say that we ought to use simple language, I am really saying too much; there is no reason why we should use any language at all. Since God knows every thought which passes through our minds, the use of words in our prayer is designed for our sakes, not for his; it's just because we want to be sure that such and such a consecrated formula has been repeated in full. And when we are approaching him in the intimacy of our own private prayer, I think he likes it as well as anything else, because it shows more confidence in his understandingness, if we remain silent before him, and let our silence do him honour. No need, even, that any special train of ideas should be passing through our minds, that we should be setting out, even in our silent thoughts, any formula of petition. To keep quiet in his presence, letting our hearts go out to him in utter confidence, in appealing love, in a tender sense of our own unworthiness—that, no less than any formula of words, and perhaps more than any formula of words, is what is really meant by prayer. Nor let it be supposed that prayer of this kind, unformulated, inarticulate prayer of this kind, is barren of all intercessory value. If we will believe what our Lord told us about intercession, there are only two dispositions essential to it. One is faith, the confidence that he can do what we ask of him if he wills. The other is patience, the conviction that if he does not give it us, it is because he wants us to go on asking. And, saving the better judgement of the Church, I don't think we are likely to prevail with God by going through a long rigmarole of petition, appealing to him now by this title, now by that. Oh, it is all very well for public, liturgical intercession. But when we are alone with him, I think he likes us to approach him in the child's way: "My God, there's something I want, and I want it badly; you know what it is. I expect it wouldn't be good for us, or you'd have given it us by now. But, just in case you were waiting for me to ask for it—well, I am asking for it; so you'll know what to do."

I have said that your prayer ought to be your own prayer; but meanwhile, even in that intimacy of prayer in which the soul rejoices to be alone with God, we are not meant to forget that we have duties towards other people, that we belong to a Church. That's why I think it is good for us to have the habit of reciting the Holy Rosary, as the weapon of prayer that is common to all sorts and conditions of men in Holy Church. You may not find the recitation of it comes natural to you—the repetitions oppress you with a sense of monotony; you cannot concentrate on the mystery because you are thinking the words of the prayer. Well, I should be untrue to all I have been saying in this meditation if I suggested that you had a duty of saying the Holy Rosary at frequent intervals, if you have to say it reluctantly. But if you can make room for it in your scheme of life, it has got just this advantage; it serves to unite you in spirit with your Catholic friends everywhere, with prisoners in concentration camps, with the sick and suffering who can't remember any prayers except the Our Father and the Hail Mary; it may be wearisome, to feel those links slipping one by one between your hands, but somehow, those links form a bond. You put yourself in touch with the mainstream of Catholic life, when you take up the Holy Rosary.

I know what you have been wanting to tell me all the time. You have been wanting to say, "What is all this about finding that one form of prayer comes easier to you than another, comes more natural than another? With me (you say) all prayer is somehow an effort and a burden; I never feel at ease in God's presence—indeed, I never feel as if I was in God's presence; I have to fall back upon faith, and go on telling myself that I am. Does it matter, then, what kind of prayer I use?" Well, it is quite possible that God is exercising your faith in this way; he often does that, even with souls which are honestly trying to serve him. And if that is really the state of the case, there is no more to be said—safest, perhaps, to stick to liturgical prayers, indulgenced prayers, follow as best you can in the beaten track of Catholic piety. Only, make sure first that things are really as you represent them. Sometimes, when we complain that prayer comes difficult to us, it is only because we have not been adventurous enough in exploring the possibilities of it; we have allowed ourselves to get into a rut of formal pieties, and he wants us to strike out a little and make our own experiments. He wants us to use the liberty of the spirit and come to him boldly, as his children, choosing the prayer that suits us best.

XXII

THE HOLY ROSARY

The Holy Rosary—yes, the Holy Rosary—has become so much part of the furniture of our lives as Catholics that we are, I think, in some danger of taking it too much for granted, and forgetting, a little, what it means. Your rosary is one of the things you are apt to lose, or to break; one of the things you will leave behind, if you are not careful, when you go away for the night; it takes rank with your pipe or your spectacle-case as something you forget to bother about except when it is not there. And even in the use of it we are apt to fall into a rut; we have our own rules about saying it, and we feel, sometimes, that it is the sort of devotion which causes us more scruples when we forget to say it than comfort when we remember to. So it is just as well that it should have its feast every year, and its month every year, to remind us about it and tell us that it is really important. It is the only inanimate thing, save only the Holy Cross, which has a feast all of its own in the Calendar of the Universal Church.

Well, then, let us remind ourselves of the obvious things about it; you will hardly expect to hear anything original about a contrivance so simple, which has been in vogue all over Christendom these centuries back. First of all, let us remind ourselves that it is a meditation. When the emperor Darius invaded Scythia, five hundred years before Christ, he made a bridge of boats over the River Danube; and on the day when he crossed over, he tied sixty knots in a rope, and said to the people who were left in charge of the bridge,

"Untie one of these knots every day; and when you have got to the end of them break up the bridge. Because if I am not back by that time it will mean that I shall never come back at all." He didn't want to have any mistake made about the counting, so he tied knots in a rope. And ever since his time, and probably before his time, people have used knots in a piece of string, or beads threaded on string, to help them count—especially when they were saying their prayers, because when we say our prayers we like to devote our whole attention to it, and there is nothing in the world that distracts one's attention so much as counting. Beads of one kind or another have been used in this way from very early times, both by Christians and by people of other religions. But the distinctive thing about the Holy Rosary is that it is not meant to consist merely of the repetition of Our Fathers and Hail Marys; you are meant to meditate while you are doing it.

There is no need to be scrupulous about this. You satisfy the intentions of the Church, sufficiently to gain the indulgence, however you say the Rosary—even if you do not think about the mysteries at all. But what the Church wants us to do is not merely to repeat so many prayers, though to be sure there would be no harm in that. She wants us to think about the fifteen mysteries; the beads are to occupy our fingers, the prayers are to occupy our lips, and leave our minds free to meditate; every Rosary is a meditation. Some people don't find that is the best way; they prefer to meditate in silence, or they prefer to choose a wider range of subjects. There is no harm in that; only, I think, it is a bad thing to turn up your nose altogether, and say that the Rosary is only meant for very simple and rather unspiritual people, that it is no use to really well-instructed Christians like you. It is good for us all, sometimes, to say the Rosary together with our neighbours; it is good for us sometimes to recite it privately, even if our attention wanders all the time, even if it makes us feel rather sleepy; because, as I reminded you in the last meditation, by saying it, we identify ourselves with the great mass of Christian people, learned and simple alike, who are performing the same act of devotion all over the world.

When we say the Rosary, then, we are meditating, or trying to meditate, or meditating a little by flashes. And the subject is the Incarnation of our Lord Jesus Christ. I think the reason why it was given to the Dominican Order to spread this devotion among the faithful was that the Dominican Order was raised up to combat the heresies of medieval Europe. And while the history of those heresies is very obscure, so that it is difficult now to determine how much the outbreaks in different parts of Europe were connected together or were derived from a common source, one point is always cropping up everywhere; these heretics denied that our Lord took human flesh of his Mother. They regarded matter as something in itself evil, and they could not be brought to believe that the Son of God took upon himself human flesh and was born after the manner of man. Accordingly, it was the Incarnation that had specially to be preached in medieval Europe; and the Incarnation is the string which binds all the beads of the rosary together. Oh, it's quite true, we talk about our Lady's Rosary, and it is in her honour that we perform the devotion; but it is not her life we are meant to think about especially; it is the life of her Divine Son. The meeting of things human with things divine—that is the point of the Incarnation, and that is the point of the Holy Rosary. Things human meeting with things divine, when God becomes a little child for our sakes. Things human meeting with things divine, when he undergoes for us, the eternal, the impassible, man's sentence of suffering and of death. Things human meeting with things divine, when first his sacred humanity and then his redeemed storm the citadels of eternity. Could we have any better advertisement of that than the Holy Rosary itself? What, a string of beads, cheap little bits of wood and of wire—what is this but a child's toy? And yet those beads, as they rattle between our fingers, are freighted with grace, full of a sacred influence whose effects last on into eternity! So your non-Catholic friends will exclaim; but this at least we can answer, if we care to answer at all, that the idea of an indulgence attached to the use of a child's toy is not nearly so extravagant, not nearly so staggering, as the doctrine of the Incarnation—the Second Person of the eternal Trinity dwelling, personally, in a human being.

We meditate on our Lord's Incarnation, and under three aspects; you may think of the Holy Rosary as a musical composition in three moods. And those three moods are labelled respectively, as we know, joy, sorrow, and glory. Joy, because our Lord's Incarnation brought joy to the whole earth; sorrow, because it brought sorrow to him and to his Blessed Mother; glory, because it redounded to his glory and to hers—and to ours in the fruits which it produces. And these three moods of the Incarnation are also, if you come to think of it, the three characteristic moods of human experience. Joy, because life itself is joy; sorrow, because all life is interpenetrated with sorrow; glory, because the purpose of that sorrow and its outcome, if we make right use of it, is a crown of glory. Joy, sorrow, glory, as if you were to say life, death, and eternity—all that forms part of our meditations, when we use the Holy Rosary.

We talk of the joy of living, and indeed life itself is an enjoyment; it is better to exist than never to have been. That, the pagans knew; and one of the most successful figures in the pagan world, Caius Maecenas, the confidential friend of the emperor Augustus, wrote a poem in which he says that life is worth while, even if it is combined with every form of disadvantage; preserve life for me, he says, even if I am fixed to a sharp cross. He would rather live crucified than not live at all. The joy of life is something which grows to a climax and then falls away, becomes less intense, as youth passes into old age. So in the joyful mysteries you will notice that the central mystery comes in the middle; the birth of our Lord at Bethlehem is the climax. And, at the same time, it would be foolish not to recognize it; all our human experience is shot with sorrow. I say, shot with sorrow, for indeed life is like a garment of shot silk, which takes on a different colour according to the angle from which you look at it; it is both tragedy and comedy. But sooner or later, even in the most careless of lives, it is tragedy that will make itself felt most and occupy the centre of the stage. All the diseases and the discomforts and the bereavements which we suffer are only preparation, as it were, for the grand finale, which is death; they lead up to it, take its sting from it in some measure by preparing the way for it. And accordingly, you will find that in the sorrowful mysteries of the Holy Rosary it is the last, the death and Crucifixion of our Lord, that forms the climax. Life grows in intensity till middle age, and then becomes fainter and more feeble; the shadow of death deepens all the time, closes round our lives till it is a curtain covering all.

And this triumph of sorrow over joy, this relentless encroachment of mortality upon the bright experience of life, would be intolerable to us if that were all—if there were no third act in the drama, no final mood in the melody. But life is not all joy and sorrow; glory has its place there; and, if life is lived as it ought to be lived, the light of glory grows upon us in proportion as the world's sun is nearer to its setting. Eternity—man delivered at last from this patchwork alternation of joy and sorrow, and finding his true medium at last in the endless contemplation of God. Here, there is no alternation and no progress; heaven once achieved, all is achieved, and whatever freedom, whatever happiness it brings with it springs from the mere fact of assured redemption. Accordingly, in the five glorious mysteries you will not find that the central mystery is in the middle, as with life, or at the end, as with death; the central mystery, our Lord's Resurrection, is the first of all the five glorious mysteries and carries the sure promise of the rest with it.

And so he helps us to understand the meaning of these three constitutive elements of human experience, joy, sorrow, and glory, by becoming man and sharing our human lot. He shows us, in the five joyful mysteries, the five great qualities of the soul that make for joy, for its attainment and for its preservation—and this, not in his own Person, but in the Person of his Blessed Mother. It was not to find joy that he came into the world. But he brought joy with him into the world and brought it first of all to her, to whom it belonged as of right because she was his Mother. Next he shows us, in the five sorrowful mysteries, five different kinds of suffering which we must expect to have in this life of our probation—this time in his own Person, for he came into the world to suffer. He shows us what kind of sufferings he will expect us to endure for him, because they are the sufferings he has endured for us. And finally he shows us, in the glorious mysteries, five aspects or elements of that complete fulfilment of our whole natures which we shall experience, please God, in heaven. And these he shows us both in his own Person, and in the person of his Blessed Mother, and in the persons of all the saints for whom glory is laid up hereafter.

The five joyful mysteries—a list of the five qualities that make for abiding joy. And the first of these is entire submission to God's will. "Behold the handmaid of the Lord, be it unto me according to thy word", our Lady says—no further questioning about the mystery of that process by which she, though remaining a Virgin, is to become a Mother; all that she leaves to God. No anxious forebodings about the afflictions which such a motherhood will bring with it; all that she leaves to God. No hesitations, no doubts, no demands for a sign; it is God's will, therefore it is hers. And I hope there is no need to insist, before a Christian congregation, on the necessity of submission to God's will as the antecedent condition of all true happiness. Such frail stuff it is, this happiness of ours; so unskilful are we in knowing what will be best for us, so fickle in growing weary to-day of what delighted us yesterday—we can only be sure of getting what we really want if our will is God's will, for his will is creative and cannot fail of its effect. And next, (the Visitation) unselfishness; the angel has mentioned that her cousin Elizabeth is to have a son in her old age; to congratulate *her*, then, and to be of assistance to *her*, is our Lady's first thought; she arose with haste. And you have not lived very long if you have not yet realized that the more unselfish a life is, the more chance it has of being a happy one. Next, humility; this virtue indeed is shown above all in the Child of Bethlehem, but also in his Mother—content with a stable for her nursery; and this, too, falls into place, for pride is the greatest of all enemies to happiness. Then, in the Presentation, he shows us gratitude; all happiness is incomplete which has not learned to recognize the source from which it flows and to return, thanks to God. And last (the Finding in the Temple), patience; if we have not learned to wait for God's blessings, and to be content while he withholds them, we shall have spoiled them all before they come to us by frittering away our time in regrets.

The five sorrowful mysteries—a list of the five kinds of suffering which he endured for us, which he wants us to be ready to endure for him. First, mental suffering of every kind, fear, anxiety, disappointment, disillusionment, the extreme of nervous fatigue; all *that* he felt in the garden as far as Incarnate God could feel it, so that when we feel it in our turn we may unite our sufferings with Gethsemani. Then, bodily suffering; the lash curling round those innocent shoulders, lest the agonies of Crucifixion itself should not be enough to assure us how he has suffered, how he has loved us. Then, humiliation; the Incarnate Wisdom of God treated as a madman, dressed up in a garb of ridicule, the King of Kings insulted by a mock coronation. And we, creatures of earth, who have such little ground for pride in any case, do we give way to pride after that? Do we stand on our dignity after that? Next, bodily exhaustion. Work is part of our human birthright, because it is part of the curse incurred by human sin; sons of Adam, we toil because we must. But when the second Adam willingly takes upon his shoulders the weight that is to be his martyrdom, the curse is turned to a blessing; whatever strain we undergo, it should be light to us, while we can reflect that we are helping, like Simon of Cyrene, to carry a Cross. And last, death itself, with whatever of pain and of dereliction may come before it; even that, because it falls to the lot of all men, the Son of man will taste for us beforehand and assure us that all is well.

The five glorious mysteries—a list of five elements which must contribute to the eternal glories of heaven. The Resurrection—that stands for life; real life, life with all its instincts unmarred and all its activities unhampered, awakening to a world in which man will be at home, as the brute beasts are at home in this world where man lives as a stranger. The Ascension stands for the elevation of all our capacities and all our aspirations so that we shall be fit to enjoy God. You wonder, sometimes, whether heaven can really be a fulfilment of all our hopes, when it means that we must leave so many familiar comforts, so many agreeable occupations, behind us; don't worry about that, don't worry for a moment about that. Of course now we cannot understand what is the happiness of heaven; we should be in heaven if we could. The descent of the Holy Spirit stands for union with God, a union which has already begun in us, since we became members of his Church. We have his love already abiding in us, a spark kindled by the tongues of fire that appeared on the Day of Pentecost; but it is a smouldering spark here; it will not blaze up till we see God; then for the first time we shall realize how we are united by charity to him. And the Assumption stands for reunion with all those we loved—with earthly friends whose companionship we enjoyed, with the saints whose patronage and protection we have experienced. And the Coronation stands for the reward of all our striving—the glory that will be ours, something that is spoiled and made ridiculous if we try to think of it in earthly terms, but will be ours, in heaven, none the less, will be a part of our blessed eternity none the less.

May he, whose only begotten Son by his life, death, and Resurrection has purchased for us the reward of eternal life, grant that we, meditating on these mysteries with the most Holy Rosary of the Blessed Virgin Mary, may both imitate what they contain and obtain what they promise.

XXIII

SAINT MARY MAGDALEN

Saint Mary Magdalen is held up to us by the Church as a model of the contemplative life. It is natural that this should be so, because the virtues we connect with her name are all interior virtues. It was her sister, Saint Martha, that busied herself with active work, with providing food for our Lord when he was hungry, rest for him when he was tired. For Saint Mary Magdalen, it was enough to sit at the feet of her Beloved, to listen and to adore—for her, the interior virtues. She is the heroine of contrition; and contrition does not, of itself, alter the external fact of our sins; it only alters our attitude towards them. She is the heroine of resignation; and resignation does not help us to do anything; it only helps us to suffer, with patience, those bad times which will come to us whether we are patient over them or no. She is the heroine of hope; and hope does not change the course of the world's history; it only enables us to look forward, in a dark hour, to God's promise that the course of history will yet be changed. Let us recall to ourselves three scenes, three vignettes from Saint Mary Magdalen's life—all familiar enough, needing little in the way of commentary or of rhetorical embroidery—which show her in those three characters, as the heroine of contrition, of resignation, and of hope.

The heroine of contrition—we know that scene, in the pages of Saint Luke. Our Lord had been invited to a meal with one of the Pharisees; and this man, for some reason, had not shown him the ordinary courtesies which any guest might expect—had not washed his feet, soiled with the dust of journeying; had not poured oil on his head, parched with the midday sun. Perhaps it was because our Lord himself, notoriously, did not care much about all these ceremonies that had to be gone through before you sat down to a meal; he thought they were overdone. Very well then, Simon, the Pharisee, would teach him a lesson; no courtesies should be wasted on him. They sat down to eat, and a strange interruption occurred. A woman came in, known to the guests as one who lived a life of sin; without a word to anybody, she crouched down at our Lord's feet, washed them with her tears, wiped them with her hair, poured ointment on his head. That this woman was Saint Mary Magdalen is not certain, but the Church's tradition warrants us in believing it; after all, the Gospel at Saint Mary Magdalen's Mass tells the story of the unnamed woman at the banquet, and how she washed our Lord's feet.

It wasn't on this occasion that our Lord said "She has done what she could", but he might have said it. A few tear-drops sprinkled here and there don't go far, when all is said and done, to wipe off the stains of travel; don't bring much relief, when all is said and done, to feet that are tired and swollen after long hours of journeying. So far as his body was concerned, I don't suppose our Lord felt much easier for this strange, this rather embarrassing tribute that had been paid him. No, but it was a gesture: the penitent had done what she could. The Pharisee had been lacking in courtesy of intention, and that was inexcusable. The host had not done the honours of the occasion: somebody else must do them instead. Somebody, whose need and experience of forgiveness was greater than his, must complete the omitted ceremony. "Lord, here are my tears, that flow so grudgingly, but they are something. My hair, a rough towel, is all the towel I have. This ointment, not worthy of you, is the best anointing I can give you. With me, the intention at least has not been lacking: I have done what I could."

What is the exact connexion between that incident, and a similar incident, later in our Lord's life, when he was anointed a second time, just before his Passion, by a woman who, this time, is mentioned by name as Mary? We cannot be certain: it is the habit of the Evangelists to give us a picture here, a picture there, and leave us to find out for ourselves what was the connexion between them. It is simplest, I think, to suppose that she was deliberately reconstructing the scene of that earlier event in her history, this time in a different setting, in a different context, with a different significance. She felt—I will not say she knew, but she felt—that a tragedy was impending. It is a curious fact that the apostles, although our Lord had expressly prophesied, in their hearing, three times, the circumstances of his Passion, were nevertheless taken by surprise when it came. Our Blessed Lady, I suppose, foresaw the Passion: the shadow of it had been hanging over her, ever since Simeon made his prophecy in the Temple. I doubt if anyone else knew what was going to happen on Good Friday. But Saint Mary Magdalen, if she did not know, had a presentiment which told her that death threatened the Master she so loved. And she did what she could. At the time when she was converted from a life of sin, she had parted with all of her fine clothes, her jewelry, everything that belonged to, and could remind her of, a guilty past. She would not even touch the money that was given her in exchange for them; it must be handed over to the poor. But she had made one exception: there was a pot of ointment she had which was a thing of real value; even in those days, when money bought more than it does now, she would have been given fifteen pounds for it. But no, this particular piece of finery she would keep by her: if you had asked her why, perhaps she could not have told you. Only she had the instinct that one day it would be wanted.

And now, in Holy Week, the moment has come; Jesus of Nazareth is her guest, and there is something about his demeanour, a sadness, perhaps, in his look, a valedictory note in his utterances, which seems to imply that he is her guest for the last time. She will not let him go without one final gesture of hospitality. How much her mind went back to that past scene, how much she noticed that precious ointment of that kind was only suitable for embalming the dead, we cannot be certain. We only know that she anointed our Lord once again: that she was rebuked by Judas for wasting the precious liquid, which might have been sold with so much benefit to the poor, and that our Lord defended her. He did more than defend her: he would have it set down as part of the unalterable deposit of the Christian religion, that she had been right. Once again, she had done what she could: doomed to lose her Master by death, she had resigned herself—she, who so loved him—to the loss, and had attested her resignation by anointing his body, still warm and breathing, against its sojourn in the corroding tomb.

And there is a third scene in her life, equally famous. Our Lord's appearance after his Resurrection to Saint Mary Magdalen is the only one of his Resurrection appearances which is guaranteed to us by the authority of all four Gospels alike. At the same time, only Saint John has given us the details of it. And I think as we read his account, we all feel faintly puzzled by Saint Mary Magdalen's attitude, just as we did by her attitude in Holy Week. She does not, evidently, expect our Lord to rise from the dead—or why does the sight of the empty tomb give her no inkling of what has happened? But if that is so, why is she so concerned about the safety of our Lord's dead body? Why is she in such a desperate hurry to anoint it with her spices, as if any delay might make her lose the chance altogether? Why is it such a complete tragedy to her, when she thinks the body has been stolen? The Jews did not, like their heathen neighbours, attach a superstitious importance to the exact performance of funeral ceremonies. "If you believe in the Resurrection" (we want to say to her), "why are you so surprised at finding the tomb empty? If you don't believe in the Resurrection, why is it so desperately important to you whether the tomb is empty or not?"

But, you know, we are being too logical with her. It is an instinct that drives her on: she wants to find her Master, living or dead. She will not give up hope altogether, until she is parted from the form she loves. To anoint those limbs once more, even though now they should be cold and lifeless to the touch, is all she asks: she will do what she can. She will make a gesture, even if it is only a frustrated gesture, in token of her love. Oh, be sure she has not yet learned perfectly the craft of loving. Our Lord himself tells her that, when he appears to her and says, "Do not cling to me like this: I have not yet ascended to my Father's side." She must learn to do without the comfort of his physical presence, to love him, to worship him, in spirit and in truth. But if she has not yet learned her lesson perfectly, how much farther advanced she is than we, who have the whole accomplished scheme of revelation before our eyes! She has learned to go on loving when it seemed as if hope itself was dead.

The heroine of contrition, the heroine of resignation, the heroine of hope. What I want to suggest, quite briefly and quite simply, is that we may find in these gestures of hers a comfort and an inspiration which we need, not seldom—a comfort and an inspiration for our own feeble, half-hearted gestures, when those three internal attitudes, of contrition, of resignation and of hope, come difficult to us.

How difficult it is, sometimes, to feel certain that there is anything important in being sorry for our sins! *Our* sins—in a world where God is so openly defied, where his laws are so frequently and so deliberately broken, can it really make much difference whether I, this one, undistinguished creature of his, am sorry to have taken part in a world-wide conspiracy against him? Can it really interest him to be told, week after week or month after month, that I have been guilty of backbiting, of ill temper, of telling small lies? If we would be honest with ourselves, I think many of us would admit that what really disheartens us about our sins is not the greatness of them but the littleness of them: they are so mean, so petty; we are almost ashamed to admit that our lives, even when they are lived amiss, are lived on so unheroic a level. And as with our sins, so it is with the regret which we feel for our sins. We go on telling God, in consecrated formulas, that they have deserved his dreadful judgements, and so on; but those formulas have been staled for us by familiarity: we have used them so often, and even when we thought they were pronounced in all sincerity at the time, how miserably we were undeceived by the experience of speedy relapse into the old bad habits! Unimportant people, sinning dull sins and repenting of them, month after month, so ineffectually—we are dogged by a sense of unreality which threatens to spoil all freshness in our approach to Almighty God.

Yes, but remember those words, the most comforting, I sometimes think, which ever fell from the lips of the world's Comforter: "She has done what she could." When you kneel in the confessional, imagine to yourself that what you see in front of you is not the grille of the confessional, but our

Lord's own feet, those feet so tired of tramping through the world and finding no rest anywhere, no welcome anywhere. Put the world away from your thoughts, as the poor Magdalen put away from her the thought of all those great people sitting round the dinner table: you and he are alone together, and you want to tell him that here, at least, there is no false shame; here at least there is no cold, jealous criticism of his dealings with mankind. Tears you have none to shed, but the very dryness of your eyes is a fresh motive for sorrow. You are doing what you can; it is little, it is miserably little, but he knows you too well to be surprised at that. He will not complain about your lack of contrition, if he sees you wishing you were more contrite than you are.

And so let it be with our resignation—how hard it is to tell God that we are leaving everything in his hands, and to mean it! Not so much, perhaps, when some immediate danger is hanging over us that we can foresee and reckon with: the loss, it may be, of somebody we love, or the prospect of bodily suffering; but that vague feeling of unrest which comes over all of us when we live in unsettled times and cannot picture, with any confidence, either our own future or the future of the world we have grown accustomed to. To leave this or that in God's hands, when we have done everything man can do—that, perhaps, is not so difficult. But to leave *everything* in God's hands, to go about our own work and fulfil our own allotted task without casting nervous eyes around us at the dark portents of our time, needs a higher effort of resignation. We must think of the Magdalen, still in the dark, like those others, about what the future would bring or the meaning of what it brought, yet obeying her own instinct of doing all that lay in her to reconcile herself to God's will and to meet it half-way. She took the one precious possession she had kept to remind her of the past—broke the jar, precious itself, spilt the ointment, still more precious, in reckless profusion, as a symbol of her utter willingness to throw away everything at her Master's feet. It was only a gesture, only a token sacrifice—but she had done what she could. What *we* can do will be very little; we shall always find that there are nervous shrinkings, that there are reserves and conditions at the back of our minds, when we tell God that we know his way is best and we want his will to happen. But we must do what we can to force our wayward minds into that attitude, and he will be content; he does not ask the impossible.

And so let it be with our hope. Hope and resignation at first sight are opposites: hope bids us expect the best; resignation would have us prepare for the worst. But in reality the subject-matter of the two qualities is quite different: resignation warns us to avoid the self-torment of worrying; hope denies us access to the luxury of despair. To despair, to throw in your hand completely, bow your head to fate, and tell yourself that things could not be worse, that nothing can possibly matter now—I don't know whether that attitude is possible, in its out-and-out form, except to the unfortunate man who decides to take his own life. But to let ourselves be hampered, to let our energies be half-crippled and our usefulness half-undermined by listening, now and again, to the counsels of despair—that is much commoner. Of one thing we are strictly forbidden to despair: our own salvation. However often we fall, whatever sense of unworthiness we feel, we must still, under pain of God's severe judgement, keep our heads pointing upstream. But the quality of hope in a Christian mind overflows into other channels. Friends of ours seem to have made an utter mess of their lives, seem, in the cant phrase, "Past praying for". Beware of that cant phrase: nothing is ever past praying for. To go on praying: to go on, if need be, showing readiness to lend a helping hand where there is the least chance of reclamation—that is a proper exercise of the Christian virtue of hope. Some country, some class of people, seems to have fallen into the grip of a tyranny from which it can never emerge: still we must go on praying; we must not admit for a moment that God's arm has grown short, or that God's purposes can be defeated. It is a paradoxical thing altogether, this virtue of hope. It is only when it seems unreasonable to expect such and such a result that hope comes into play and bids us expect such and such a result without reason, even beyond reason itself. So it was with Saint Mary Magdalen on Easter morning: she would not give up, she would go on behaving as if everything was bound to come right, even when there was no human ground for supposing that anything could ever come right again. In our bad times, when we are tempted to throw in our hands and write off such and such a human tragedy, such and such a lost cause, as if it were a bad debt, let us think of Saint Mary Magdalen as she went about on that spring morning, with all the tragedy of Good Friday in her eyes, and all the dauntless courage of Easter on her brow. Our hope, like our contrition, like our resignation, may be a poor performance; we shall face the world, at best, with a forced smile and a sick feeling at the heart. But once again God will give us credit for it, if we brace our resolution as best we can. Once again, our lives will be the subject of that satisfying epitaph, written by the finger of Omniscience: "Let her alone: she has done what she could."

XXIV

OUR LADY'S SERENITY

I want to give you, from one particular angle, a human picture of our Lady, drawn from real life; that is, drawn from the Gospels, which are the only trustworthy evidence we have. As a rule, when we meditate about our Blessed Lady, we consciously dramatize; her pictures, her statues, the sort of romantic devotion she has inspired in the poetry of so many ages, encourage us to treat her as a symbol, rather than as a personality with personal traits, such as all human beings must have. We forget, for example, that she was a Jewess, and that probably as a matter of fact her beauty was of a more or less Jewish type—why shouldn't it be? No reason at all why it shouldn't be, but somehow the suggestion sounds vaguely blasphemous, simply because Fra Angelico and Raphael drew her from Gentile models. We never picture her, again, carrying a jug of water on her shoulder; it must have been a common enough sight, in first-century Nazareth, but it sounds wrong, because the pious statues have made us think of her carrying a rosary, as she did at Lourdes, instead of a great heavy jug of water. Again, it's perfectly possible that, like Saint Peter, she talked with a bit of a Galilean brogue, not in the best style of Jerusalem. But we were rather shocked when Bernard Shaw made Saint Joan of Arc talk the Lancashire dialect; and we instinctively think of our Blessed Lady as a Queen, dressed like a Queen and talking like a Queen; the very idea that a smart person like Herodias or Herodias' daughter would have addressed her as "my good woman", and found her speech and manners as homely as those of any other Nazareth girl seems all wrong, somehow; and yet it's probably true.

I am not, I need hardly say, trying to shock you in this meditation, or give you some fresh, original picture of what our Lady must have seemed like to her contemporaries. I am only going to draw attention to one human quality in her which stands out from her portrait in the Gospels, side by side with all those heavenly privileges we have meditated on so often. It is a quality I will call serenity. It depends, of course, upon the supernatural endowments she had; and especially, as we shall have occasion to remind ourselves, on her possessing the spirit of faith in an eminent degree. But I want to think of it as a human quality, reacting to human situations, expressing itself, probably, by human gestures and human lines on her face—a smile, one imagines, which perhaps came rarely, but when it did lingered on her face and threw into relief the thoughtfulness of her brow. And I think it is a useful quality for us to remember in her, because it is a quality we all need ourselves, and some of us haven't got—the great calmness of our Lady, the imperturbable way in which she meets the situations which the Gospel story has described for us.

You get it, of course, from the very start, at the Annunciation. She was bewildered, Saint Luke tells us, by the angel's message, but she waited, and listened; and when she heard what the message was, she put the obvious objection: "How can that be, since I have no knowledge of man?" Now, I may be fanciful, but it seems to me that if you compare those few words with the sort of way in which Jewish women talk in the Old Testament, Ruth, for example, or Abigail, they form a very quiet piece of comment. From Ruth or Abigail you would have got a torrent of rhetoric, bordering on hysterics, with a lot about "God do so to me and more also" in it, at such a suggestion as the one Saint Gabriel made. Our Lady simply says, "Yes, but how?" She wants to know, naturally; but she takes it very calmly after all; a Son, who will be accounted the Son of the most High—and will rule over the house of Jacob for ever; yes, to be sure, but how? Am I wrong in speaking of our Blessed Lady's *serenity*?

You might mistake it, at first sight, for mere lack of imagination; but you get a more just view of it, this serenity of hers, when Saint Gabriel has spoken again, and she answers him. "Behold the handmaid of the Lord; let it be unto me according to thy word"; joyful promises like Gabriel's, or gloomy warnings like Simeon's, are just the same to her, as long as her mind is fixed in that resolution. The angel left her, and what then? You expect to read, "Mary kept all these things and pondered them in her heart." But no; it is not the time for sitting down and thinking. Our Lady, like all very calm people, had the knack of putting first things first; and before she did anything else, there was a visit to be paid. Among all the words Gabriel had spoken to her, the most significant, surely, and the most awe-inspiring ever addressed to a human being, there was one which had particularly caught her attention—not the one that catches our attention. "Thy cousin Elizabeth also is with child"; that meant action, going to see her and be with her in her confinement; so the day-dreams had to wait. She arose with haste—not with hurry, with haste; calm people don't need to be in a hurry, because they hasten at the right moment, about the right things.

Saint Elizabeth, good holy woman, isn't calm at all; she cries out in a loud voice, "Blessed art thou among women, and blessed is the fruit of thy womb; how have I deserved to be thus visited by the mother of my Lord?" and so on.

And all this excitement on her part makes a sort of agitated antiphon to usher in the marble-like phrases of the Magnificat. Let me remind you of the canticle of Hannah, the mother of Samuel, to justify that estimate of our Lady's canticle. "My heart thrills with joy in the Lord; pride in the God I worship lifts up my head; now I can flout my enemies, happy in thy gift of redress! Who so holy as the Lord? None—there is none else; there is no stronghold can compare with our God. Boast no more, boast no more; those lips must talk in another strain; the Lord is all-knowing, and overrules the devices of men", and so on. The critics, heaven help them, will always tell you that the Magnificat is so like Hannah's song. But it isn't a bit; there may be a reminiscent phrase here and there; but the tone, the tone is all different. Hannah is triumphing over a rival, volubly, scathingly; our Lady gives you a quiet piece of devotional theology on the same theme, with her own part pushed, as far as possible, into the background. The redemption of Israel has come, that is all that matters; and even that is nothing to be *surprised* at; the thing was promised to Abraham, centuries ago. Notice how Zachary's Benedictus—and what is more pardonable than a father's pride?—all leads up to the part Saint John the Baptist is to play; the last four verses are a paean about his mission. But the Magnificat starts with our Lady herself, and leads away from the subject as soon as possible. It goes off into generalities; God has been very good to her, but then, how good God is! There is nothing surprising about it.

The scene changes, and we are at Bethlehem. Our Lady doesn't speak in this part of the story, but there is one description which gives you, I think, such a view of our Lady's serenity as nothing else does; "she brought forth a son, her first-born, whom she wrapped in his swaddling-clothes, and laid in a manger, because there was no room for them in the inn." "*And* she wrapped him in his swaddling-clothes, *and* she laid him in a manger"—that Hebrew "and" is specially designed to give you the impression that this verb is the natural consequence of the one before. She had a baby, and naturally she proceeded to wrap him in his swaddling-clothes; the thing has got to be done. Having done that, she naturally proceeded to lay him in a manger; of course, it is rather more convenient to have more elaborate appliances, but, what would you? By bad luck, the inn was full up; so one had to make the best of the stable—fortunately, with a good roomy manger in it. I don't see any reason to doubt that Saint Luke got his Gospel of the Infancy from our Lady herself; whether at first-hand or at second-hand doesn't matter; but he evidently was in Palestine while Saint Paul was in prison at Caesarea, so why not first-hand? Can't you *hear* our Lady describing the scene to him, catch her serene accents when he tells you, without comment, what kind of cradle it was that the Maker of the world had? "It was so convenient, really, with all that straw about—and very quiet, you know. It was clever of the people at the inn to think about it, wasn't it?" Our Lady is such poles apart from those agitated sisters of hers, God bless them, who are always running round in circles and complaining because everything isn't just right! And it isn't only her sisters; her brothers do it a good deal, for that matter.

So calm she is, all through; "all those who heard it were full of amazement at the story which the shepherds told them, but Mary treasured up all these sayings and reflected on them in her heart." Everybody else rushing round Bethlehem, and button-holing people with "I say, have you heard?"—and Mary is in the stable, where the shepherds have left no other trace than the meditative look in her bright mother's eyes. But there are other things to be thought of; eight days old, the boy must be circumcised; forty days old, her first-born, he must be taken up to Jerusalem to be presented in the Temple; the angels have strange stories to tell about him, but obviously one must do the obvious things. And so she finds more food for wonderment, Simeon's canticle and Simeon's prophecy, not to speak of the flight into Egypt, which Saint Luke does not mention. But they settle down at Nazareth to the common business of living; it was not till our Lord was twelve years old that anything happened which our Lady thought worth putting down in a book of reminiscences. One knows a lot of mothers, God bless them, who think their own children are so remarkable, and say such remarkable things; but our Lady, you see, takes it all very quietly. "Oh, yes", she tells Saint Luke (I picture him as an eager reporter, trying to prompt her memory)—"oh yes, there was that time he got lost on the pilgrimage; *that* made one think." And so Saint Luke gets the story of the Finding in the Temple out of her. "Seeing him, they marvelled"; one knew there must be some good reason, of course; it wasn't like him to give any anxiety. There is nothing agitated, nothing hysterical about our Lady's question; it just gives the minimum statement of the situation: "My son, why hast thou treated us so? Think, what anguish of mind thy father and I have endured, searching for thee!" And here, just as at the Annunciation, an answer is all she wants; it is an answer she doesn't profess to understand, but she only wanted to know there was one. There would be plenty of time to think it over later. "His mother kept in her heart the memory of all this"; primarily, I think, that is just Saint Luke giving you his sources, but no doubt as before there is the implication that our Lady thought it all over, and with time it became clearer to her. There are such a lot of things which do become clearer, if you let the experience of living give you the clue to them gradually, turning them over in your mind and assimilating them with the digestive juices of *prayer.*

I fancy Saint Luke got a good deal more out of her, but nothing, as we know, in which her name figures, except one story which seemed as if it was told against her; her name was even left out of the list of women who watched the Crucifixion, till Saint John gave it away after her death. Saint John has given us one other reminiscence of her, too: Cana of Galilee. If there is any truth in all I have been saying, how admirably in character that story is!—the servants at the feast bustling to and fro, with their faces getting longer and the cups emptier. Did our Lady just notice it, or did the servants come and tell her? I suppose she was the kind of person people did come and confide in when things were going wrong; a calm person is such a stand-by. Anyhow, she doesn't waste words: "They have no wine." You will remember that the sisters of Lazarus were like that; they just sent and told our Lord, "He whom thou lovest is sick", leaving Saint Augustine to supply the explanation; "It is enough that you should know; you do not abandon those you love." So here; our Lady will tell him and leave it at that, leave the problem in the best hands, the only hands that can deal with it; somehow, it will be all right. Our Lord's answer is one we always find difficult to focus right; the Aramaic idiom is untranslatable, and we cannot see the smile with which, quite certainly, it was accompanied. It was one of those teasing answers, with which our Lord used to test the faith of those he loved: Saint Peter, Saint Martha, the Syrophenician woman. "You're always at me about something!" is perhaps the nearest vivid paraphrase. Our Lady goes by the smile, not by the words; but she doesn't make any promises to the servants; she just turns and says, "Do whatever he tells you." It was her life's motto, and she preached it to the servants at Cana of Galilee, and through them to us. "Do whatever he tells you; it will be all right; you see!"

I have tried to give you a portrait of our Lady, but has it been exactly a retreat meditation? Surely a retreat meditation ought to give us hints about our own lives, and how to make the best of them? Well, I've been trying to let our Blessed Lady do that, and save me the trouble. But if you must have the T's crossed and the I's dotted, this is how I should interpret the message of her biography. "To you sometimes, as to me at the Annunciation, good news comes; news (perhaps) of some honour or privilege conferred on yourself. It may seem, to your modesty, incredible that you should have been chosen to do this, or that; there must be some mistake.... Never mind, leave it in God's hands; he knows what he is doing. Meanwhile, the opportunity is put into your hands of doing something for other people; make haste, and do it; it is an excellent antidote against unprofitable day-dreaming. You will meet people who shout congratulations at you; don't take the note from them; be content to admire, in a cool hour of reflexion, the Almighty Providence which is content to make use of such instruments as yourself. Other times will come, when you have a very different experience, when you will have to put up with discomforts, with rough and ready substitutes for the privileges, the conveniences to which you have been accustomed. You will be tempted to feel, rationally or irrationally, that other people are to blame, to wring your hands and go about protesting. Don't; make the best of what comes to hand, and thank God that what does come to hand is as good as it is. There is tragedy in all lives; and a chill of presentiment will fall over yours, now and again, as you foresee evil times coming for yourself, or for those you love. Do not give way to these imaginary despairs; leave your solicitudes to ferment in the mind, where prayer, and the experience of life, will gradually show them to you in a juster proportion. There will be times, too, when you are anxious to secure some favour from God for yourself, or more probably for other people you are interested in. And it will seem as if your prayers were going unnoticed; you will be tempted to grow fretful and to remonstrate with God as if you were being ill-treated. Don't; go on leaving things in his hands, very quietly, very serenely; he grants our requests more readily when he sees that we are not impatient in preferring them. And, in everything you do, the less you appear the better."

So I interpret her; but it is not easy advice she gives, and we must certainly have recourse to her if we are to win the grace to carry it out. Let us leave it in her hands, then, to advise us and to help us to carry out her advice; let us go to her with our troubles, our faults, our inadequacies, and put them in her hands, confident that her serene competence will know how to deal with them. She will not fail us; she has a mother's wisdom, and a mother's love.